SILVER

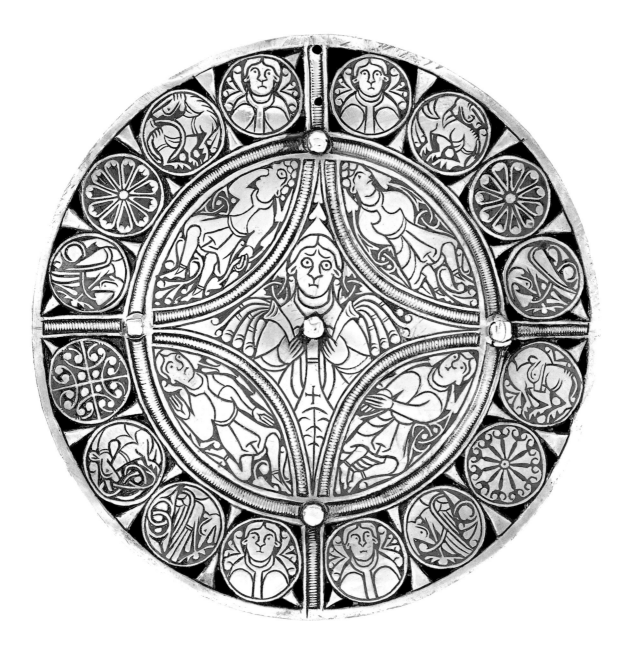

Philippa Merriman

SILVER

HARVARD UNIVERSITY PRESS
Cambridge, Massachusetts
2009

(frontispiece) The Fuller Brooch, Anglo-Saxon,
late 9th century AD. Diam. 11.4 cm.
(right) Silver libation bowl, about 300 BC.
Diam. 20.6 cm.

Philippa Merriman has asserted the right
to be identified as the author of this work

First published in 2009 by The British Museum Press
A division of The British Museum Company Ltd

Library of Congress Cataloging-in-Publication Data

Merriman, Philippa.
  Silver / Philippa Merriman.
      p. cm.
  Includes index.
  ISBN 978-0-674-03094-7 (alk. paper) 1. Silverwork. I. Title.
  NK7104.M47 2009
  739.2'3—dc22
                     2008004265

Designed by Redloh Designs
Printed and bound in Singapore by Tien Wah Press Ltd

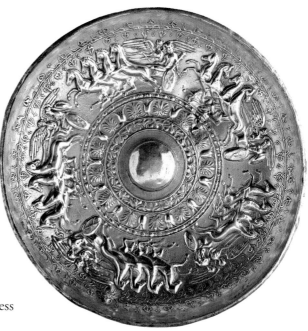

contents

Introduction

Silver has been highly valued in many societies for over five thousand years. It is beautiful and rare and though subject to corrosion, is more permanent than base metals. Its properties make it almost as desirable as gold for certain purposes: it can be cut, bent, hammered, drawn, cast, pressed and engraved with relative ease, can endure extremes of temperature, and can be highly polished to reflect light.

There is very little 'native' silver – that is, silver in an almost pure state – that can be removed from the ground and used without further processing. This is why copper and gold, for example, which frequently occur in a pure state in the earth, were identified and exploited earlier than silver.

Though small native silver deposits must have been discovered from early times, the production of silver on a significant scale did not began until much later, using tools and techniques already developed in the working of gold. By the third millennium BC the techniques for extracting silver were definitely being used in Anatolia and

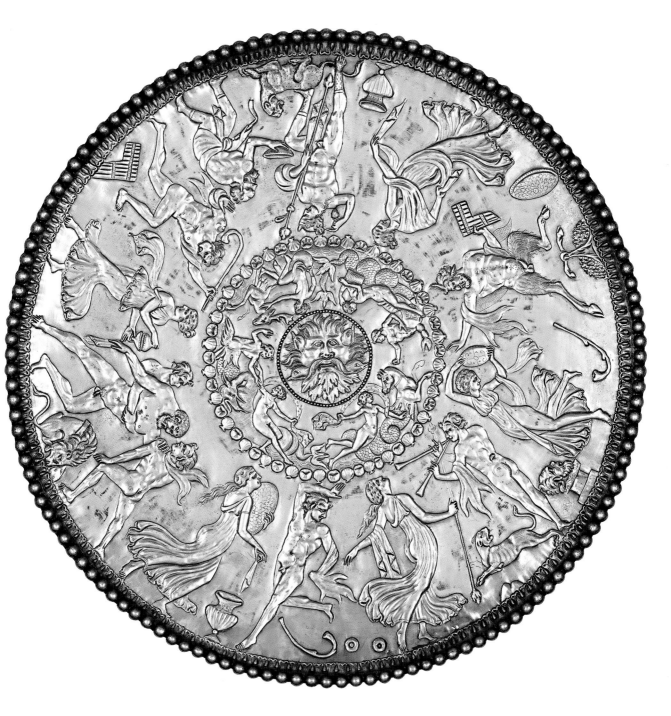

Mesopotamia, and possibly in Iran and the Greek islands. At these sites the production of silver ran alongside the production of lead, as both were extracted from mineral deposits such as galena. Extracting silver was more complex than extracting gold or copper, as it required the identification of silver-bearing ores and a ready supply of wood or charcoal for fuel. Ore-bearing rocks were heated to smelt out the lead, and the lead then re-heated to separate out the silver content. The amount of silver would depend upon the particular rock, but it would always have been a matter of extracting mere ounces from tons. As a greater understanding of ways to extract silver developed, more silver ore mines were opened and silver increased in popularity.

Ores that yield lead and silver are concentrated in particular geographical areas and the discovery of silver ores, and their subsequent mining, has often had a profound impact on local culture and economy. For example, the fact that silver occurs relatively late in Egypt and was highly valued there during the second and third millennia BC is undoubtedly due to the lack of silver-yielding ores in the area. For the early Mediterranean empires the acquisition of silver was not just a consequence of trade, it was often the motivation for it. The Phoenicians were quick to realize that silver was valued far more highly in the eastern Mediterranean than it was in Spain, and gained great profits by trading goods regarded locally as being of little value in exchange for silver from Spain. A famous example of the impact of silver mining is

Silver bull with gold inlay. Early Bronze Age, about 2350 BC. Probably from Alaca Hüyük, modern Turkey. H. 24 cm.

that of the Athenian mines at Laurium. These were exploited from at least the seventh century BC, but at the start of the fifth century a particularly rich vein of silver-yielding ore was struck. This enormous find of silver funded the growth of the Athenian navy, and created a currency respected for its purity, both of which enabled Athens to develop an empire.

Two thousand years later the Peruvians, when confronted by Europeans, characterized them as people who ate silver, such was their

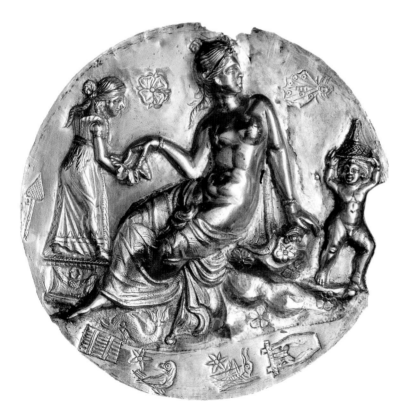

Silver medallion with Aphrodite seated on a rock. From Taranto, southern Italy, about 300–200 BC. Diam. 9.3 cm.

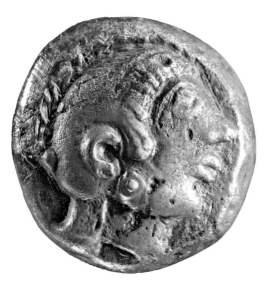

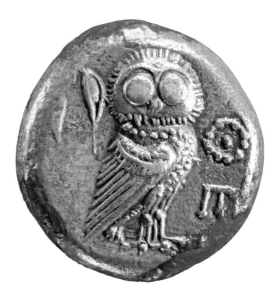

Silver tetradrachm of Athens,
around 480 BC. Diam. 2.2 cm.

desire for the metal. Indeed the European hunger for silver was, if not insatiable, at least sufficient to provoke considerable investment in the exploitation of the New World's resources. There are various estimates of Spanish production from the New World silver mines, but all agree that the volumes were enormous, far outstripping contemporary production in Europe. In their efforts to exploit this new source, the Spanish used the process of mercury amalgamation. Mercury is added to crushed silver ores and silver passes from the ore into the mercury, which is then heated until it evaporates, leaving the silver behind.

By the twentieth century most of the world's silver deposits were thought to have been discovered, which meant that increased production of silver was achieved largely through greater efficiency. The development of bulk mining methods and more advanced extraction techniques made it possible to extract silver from sources that previously were not economically viable to exploit.

Recovery and recycling has always been an important aspect of the silver trade. Silver jewellery made for specific individuals tended to be recycled rather than passed on to new owners. Early grave robbers would almost certainly have melted down their stolen silver and refashioned it into other forms. The Vikings acquired a great deal of silver through trade, especially from the Byzantine and Arab world. Such silver was chopped into smaller pieces for use as currency, known as hack-silver, or transformed into elaborate arm rings, ornaments,

Bauhaus silver tea-infuser. Designed by Marianne Brandt. Germany, around AD 1924–9. H. 7.3 cm.

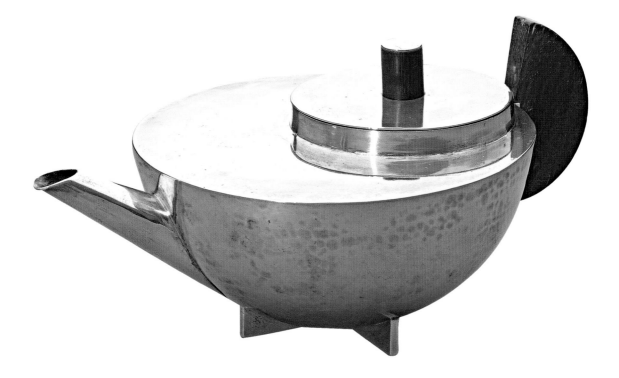

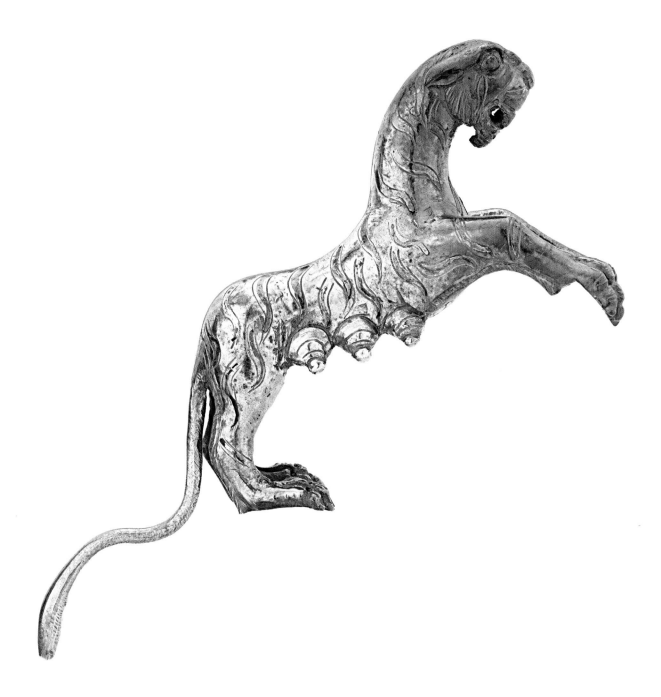

brooches and pendants. During the English Civil War (1642–51), plate was melted down, or sometimes simply chopped up and stamped, and then traded for its intrinsic value. More recently, before the development of digital photography, silver was used in large quantities in film processing and was recovered for reuse. Even now, around 10 per cent of all the silver worked in any one year will have been recycled.

The collections of the British Museum provide a rare opportunity to view the diverse uses to which this remarkable metal has been put in different cultures and at different times. Illustrated primarily by objects from the collections, this book invites the reader to notice, understand and enjoy silver a little more by looking at it in a variety of contexts: why an object has been made in silver, how it might be used, the role of silver in economic transactions, its significance as a gift and the many ways in which it was, and continues to be, a treasured commodity.

Cast silver tigress from the Hoxne Hoard. Roman Britain, buried in the 5th century AD. Found at Hoxne, Suffolk. L. 15.9 cm.

1

Value
and Wealth

Whether formed into coins or ingots, religious objects, jewellery or
tableware, silver has rarely lost its value. This connection between
silver and monetary value is reflected in many languages – for example
the Ancient Egyptian word for silver, *hedj*, came to have a meaning
similar to money, while in modern times the French word *argent*
means both silver and money, and the raising of small donations is
still known in English as a 'silver collection'. While silver itself has
possessed intrinsic value, it has also been fashioned into objects that
are aesthetically pleasing as well as useful; objects that may say a great
deal about the people who owned them.

Before the development of coinage, ancient societies found many
ways to regulate the movement of goods, including establishing
standard measures of value. Precious metals played an important part in
these measures. For example in Ancient Egypt, by the time of the New
Kingdom (1295–1069 BC), gold, silver and copper are frequently
mentioned as measures of value, and they were probably used much

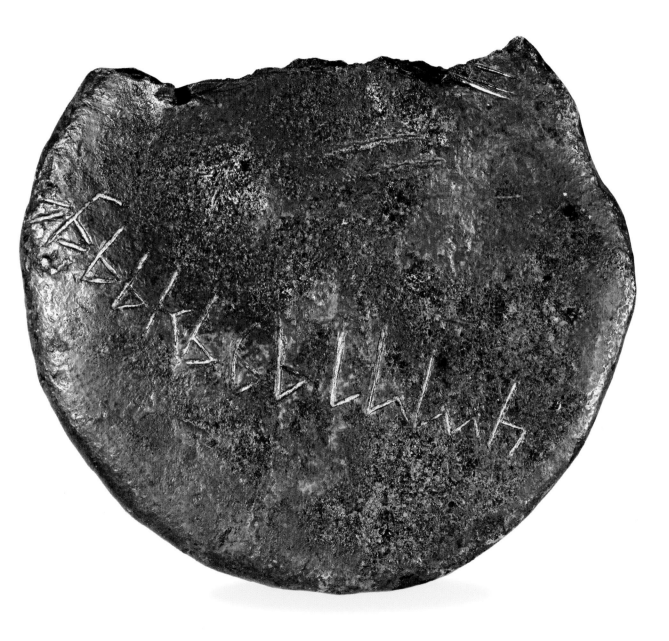

earlier. Standard weights, the *deben* and *kite*, were used in contracts, and ingots such as those found at el-Amarna weigh multiples of a *deben*.

Silver ingot from the el-Amarna Hoard, possibly representing a standard weight of three *deben* (265–286 g). 18th Dynasty, 14th century BC. Found at el-Amarna, Egypt. L. 20.8 cm.

As cultures developed more sophisticated trade patterns it must have become less convenient to use lumps of precious metal. Ingots are cumbersome and hard to divide and therefore have their limitations for small daily transactions. It is not entirely clear why coins, predominantly in silver, came to replace ingots, but perhaps they saved the trouble of weighing out silver for each transaction. It is also possible that by controlling the minting of coins, states were able to make a profit from the use of silver. The earliest known coins, made from electrum, a mixture of gold and silver, were issued by the state of Lydia (now in modern Turkey) in the seventh century BC.

The obverse of a Lydian electrum ⅙ stater with a lion's head punchmark. Minted around 650 BC, it is one of the earliest known coins. Diam. 1 cm.

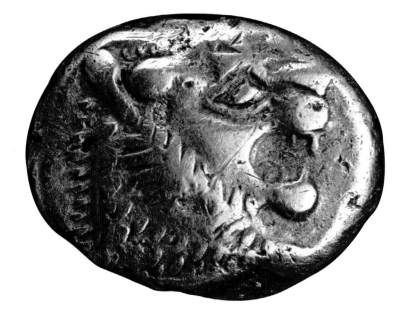

Though some coins, particularly those made in China, were cast and some, particularly those made in India, made by punch-marking designs on pieces of cut silver, most coins were, and still are, made by striking. Metal is placed between two dies and the upper (reverse) die is struck so that designs from both are impressed on the coin.

Silver coins have been minted by many states, and early examples survive from Anglo-Saxon, Chinese, Greek, Indian, Islamic, Japanese, Roman and Viking states. As demand for coinage grew, so the number of mints increased. During the fourth and fifth centuries BC a single mint might be able to supply all the coinage for a Greek city state. However, by the eleventh century AD, at least 34 mints were required to produce coins for the Anglo-Saxon kingdoms of England.

This Anglo-Saxon hoard of silver coins, discovered in Appledore, Kent, was buried around AD 1051 and contains coins from 34 different mints.

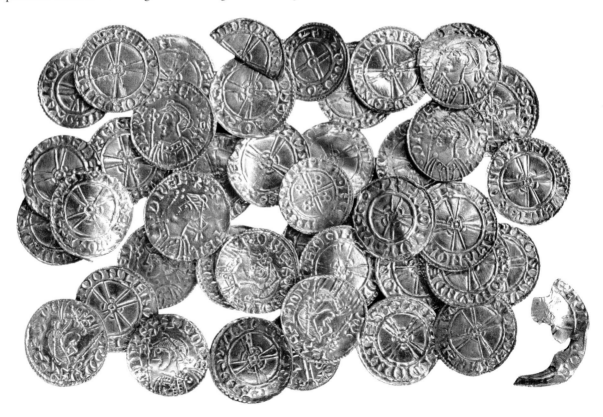

Although the use of coinage became common across the world, it did not entirely replace precious metals as currency. In Tang dynasty China (AD 618–907) coins were common but silver, often in the form of inscribed ingots, was still used for trading, paying tax, or bribing officials. Even in more recent times, after the development of global trading, with a wide variety of coinage and promissory notes circulating, there were systems that operated purely based on the weight of silver. The nineteenth-century Thai kingdom of Lanchang, for example, made use of a rather elegant silver ingot known as the 'tiger's tongue'.

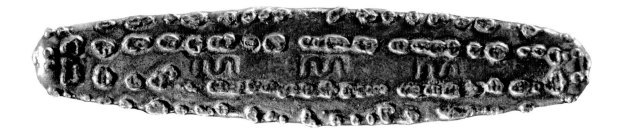

A 'tiger's tongue' silver ingot used as currency in the Thai kingdom of Lanchang (modern Laos) during the 19th century AD, long after the introduction of coins and notes around the world. L. 10.8 cm.

As the number of coins in circulation increased, the problem of maintaining the integrity of their value also increased. While coins were still made from precious metals such as silver, enterprising individuals could clip pieces from the edges, and forgers, or even unscrupulous governments, might debase the currency by adulterating precious metal with base metals. In more recent times, as their precious metal content was reduced and coins became tokens of value, design grew more and more important as a form of protecting this value. When a coin of a particular design became trusted, such as that of the Maria Theresa *thaler*, its use could spread far and wide.

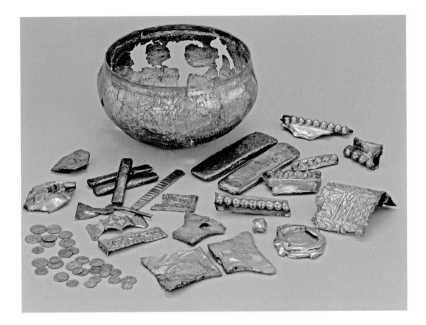

In 1741 Empress Maria Theresa of Austria introduced a new issue of the *thaler* coinage in Austria, Hungary and Bohemia, making it the unit of currency of the largest political and economic grouping in Europe at that time. The *thaler* was 39.5 mm (1½ in) in diameter and 2.5 mm (⅛ in) thick, weighed 28.0668 g (1 oz) and contained 23.3890 g (⅘ oz) of fine silver. Because it was heavy, intricate and extremely skilfully manufactured (from plentiful supplies of local Austrian silver), the coin was soon adopted by Levantine traders all over Turkey and the Middle East. As a result of its extensive use to pay for goods from the Levant it became accepted as a reliable source of silver. It became the official currency of Oman and was the only coin universally accepted in the Arab world. Since that time it has been accepted as currency along the North African coast as well as in China and the Far East, and was one of the first coins used in the United States of America, where it later gave its name to the official US currency, the dollar. Its importance was such that it continued to be struck after Maria Theresa died in 1780 (since when it has always been dated with that year). Since 1781 the mint at Vienna has struck approximately four million coins, and continues to do so as a private company even today.

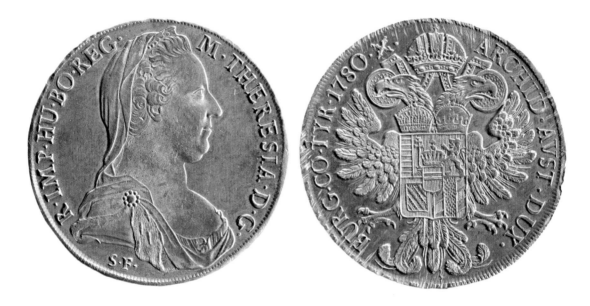

The dowry system, the payment of money or goods in connection with marriage, has existed across much of the world for centuries. In some cultures the bride brings the dowry with her to her new family, while in others it is paid by the new family to compensate for the loss of the bride to her own family. Dowries have often included jewellery, and this was usually regarded as the woman's own property, providing her with some financial independence in the event of hard times, divorce or widowhood. This is particularly true in the Middle East so it is not surprising that much Middle Eastern jewellery incorporated coins. For example Yemenite women wore *thalers*, often decorated with bells or coral, and Jewish women sometimes wore them as decoration on their traditional brocade head cover, the *gargush*. Bedouin women also wore their dowry as jewellery. As this could be added to by gifts of silver upon the births of children, jewellery became a conspicuous indication of the social status not only of the woman but also of her husband and family. There are many references to Bedouin women decked from head to toe with jewellery, silver being particularly popular.

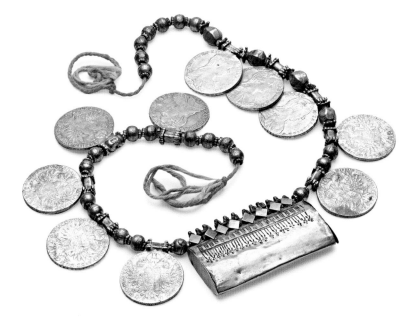

Yemeni necklace of silver-coloured metal incorporating silver *thaler* coins, AD 1947–62.

This headdress or 'money hat' (*wuqayat al-darahem*) was made in the 1840s and worn in the hills of southern Palestine in the 19th and early 20th centuries during wedding ceremonies, especially for the 'going out to the well' ceremony when the bride appeared in public as a married woman for the first time. The headdress displayed the pride and status of the family and was passed down through the generations.
H. 60 cm.

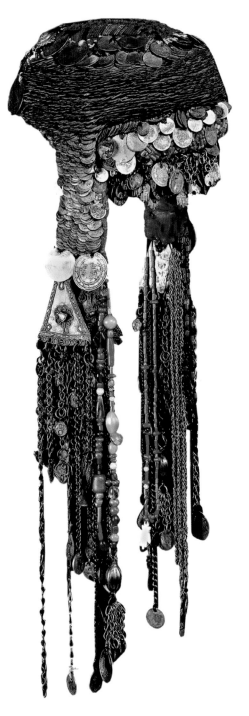

In the days when people had to keep their wealth in the form of coins and objects made of precious metal, it was difficult to keep safe, and equally difficult to move around. One solution was to hide it for safekeeping: buried in walls or under floors, or even, in times of trouble, in caves or by river banks. The owners obviously hoped to retrieve their goods, but not everyone was able to do this, especially in times of unrest or war, and so their hoarded wealth was left to be discovered, often centuries later.

The Vikings in particular measured their wealth in weight of silver and it seems it was the quality of the silver rather than the shape or condition of the objects that was important. A hoard found in Goldsborough, North Yorkshire, in 1859, which had been buried in the tenth century, contained English and Arabic coinage, ingots, broken jewellery and pieces of hacked silver. The largest Viking hoard discovered was that found in the banks of the River Cuerdale, Lancashire, in 1840. It contains over 40 kg (88 lb) of silver coins and objects made of high-quality metal in various shapes and conditions, contents similar to other known Viking hoards. The hoard was deposited sometime after AD 905, possibly by Vikings expelled from Dublin (just across the Irish Sea) in 902.

A hoard of 872 silver coins of the Iron Age Iceni tribe of East Anglia discovered in March, Cambridgeshire, in 1982. The coins date to around AD 50–70, so the hoard may have been buried because of unrest caused by the revolt of the Iceni leader Boudica against the Romans in AD 60–61.

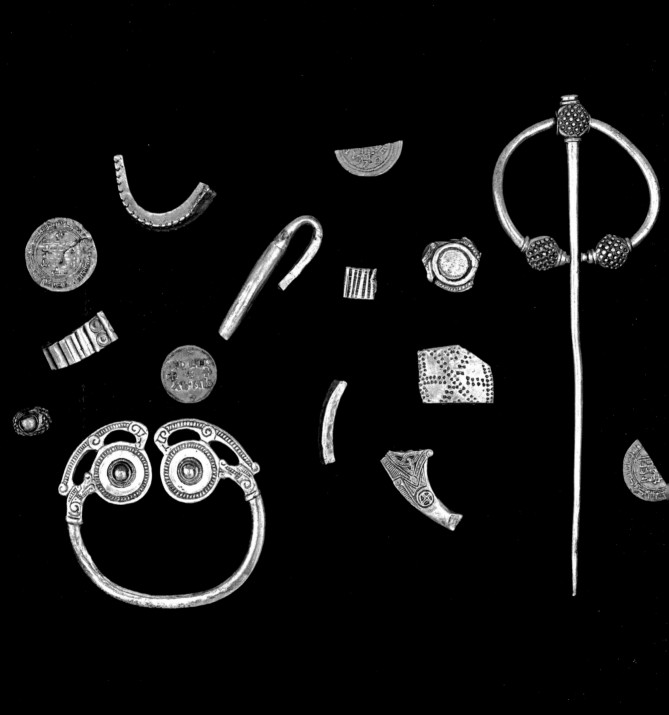

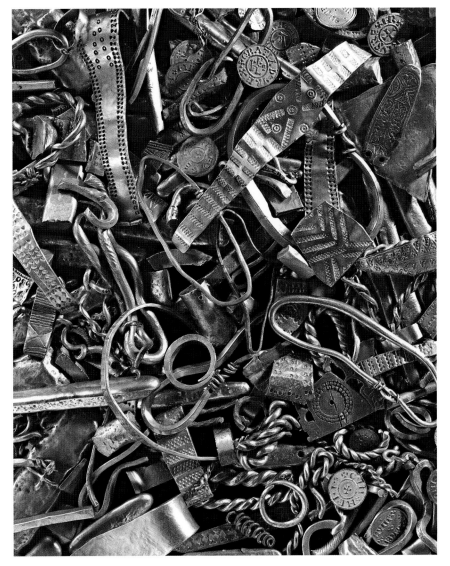

(far left) 10th-century Viking silver hoard found in Goldsborough, North Yorkshire, in 1859. It contains English and Arabic coinage, ingots, broken jewellery and pieces of hack silver. L. 19.5 cm (thistle brooch).

(left) The Cuerdale hoard, buried about AD 905, is the largest Viking Age silver hoard known from north-western Europe. It consists of over 8500 objects buried in a lead-lined chest that was found by workmen in the bank of the River Ribble, Cuerdale, Lancashire, in 1840.

Sometimes the reasons why silver was hoarded are not obvious. It may have been hidden after a theft, or perhaps buried as part of a ritual. For example, it is not known why at least eleven hoards of gold, silver and bronze neck rings (torcs) fragments and ingots, were buried at Ken Hill, Snettisham, Norfolk. Although they were carefully buried, they were not associated with graves. They were deposited sometime in the late second or early first century BC on a hill, away from farms and villages. The location is similar to those of other hoards of torcs found in East Anglia – on high ground away from areas of settlement. This suggests that the Snettisham burials were deliberately planned, perhaps for religious reasons – maybe as offerings to the gods.

One of two silver Iron Age torcs buried with ten gold torcs at Snettisham, Norfolk. After these had been covered with earth, another seven torcs were carefully packed on top. Diam. 19.5 cm.

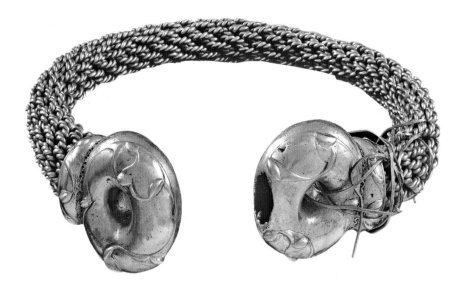

From the medieval period onwards collections of silver, known as college plate, were made by institutions such as the colleges of Oxford and Cambridge universities, the Worshipful Company of Mercers or the Royal College of Physicians. Amassed over centuries, they reflect changes in style, taste and silversmithing techniques. It may not be too fanciful to suggest that a fourteenth-century college plate collection was not unlike a modern investment portfolio.

Punch bowl and ladle presented by Sir Watkin Williams Wynn to his Oxford college in 1726.

(below) Silver trumpet given to Queen's College, Oxford, in 1666.

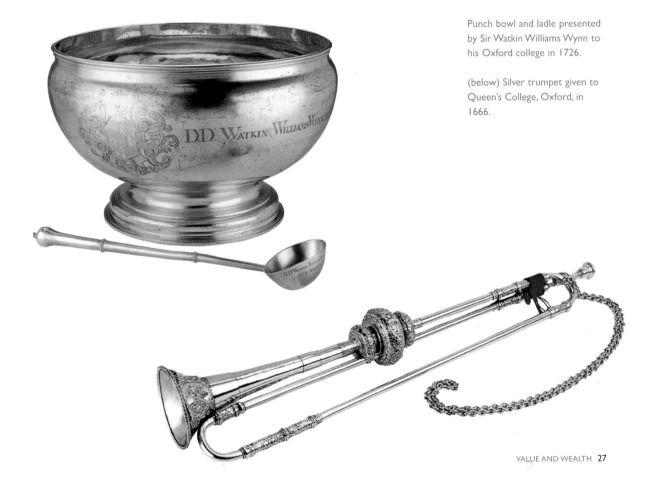

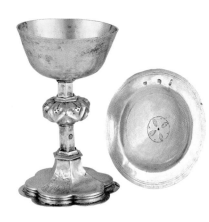

(right) Chalice and paten, hallmarked 1527–8, donated by Sir J.H.B. Noble to Magdalen College, Oxford.

(below) Drinking horn with silver-gilt mounts, donated to Queen's College, Oxford, about 1340.

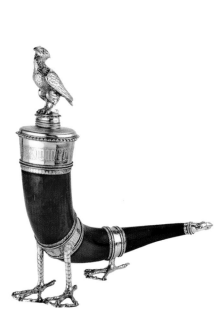

The collections were often begun by their founders and then increased by further purchases or by donations from patrons, fellows and their families, students and others associated with the institutions. The importance of these gifts was such that some of the colleges kept a Benefaction Book to record what had been given and by whom.

Queen's College, Oxford, has a drinking horn decorated in silver dating back to 1340, and like other colleges it has received additions to its collection over the centuries since then. Oxford's Magdalen College received a chalice and paten, hallmarked 1527–8, from Sir J.H.B. Noble, while in 1666 Queen's College was given a trumpet by the Secretary of State, Sir Joseph Williamson. In 1669–70 Oxford's Balliol College acquired a silver tankard with a hedgehog on it from John Kyrle to mark his matriculation.

The Mercers' Company still holds the Leigh Cup (1499 or 1512) and the Whittington spoons (around 1420) given or bequeathed by the famous Lord Mayor of London himself. This practice of donation continued well into the modern era and the Mercers' Company also owns the Sir John Watney Rosewater Dish, under the rim of which is inscribed '1935, The gift of Frank Dormay Watney, Clerk to the Mercers' Company'.

The value of these collections raised the question of how to protect such considerable and conspicuous stocks of silver. Towers and strong boxes were obviously an important method of securing the collections, and they were certainly more practical than burying it, but they were frequently no match for the might of the monarch or the government. During the period of the Reformation in the sixteenth century, much college silver associated with the Catholic communion was seized by Henry VIII (1509–47). Even during the reign of Elizabeth I (1558–1603) attempts were still made to seize items associated with the old Catholic religion. The most notable of these attempts were demands to replace the chalices with 'comely cups'. A century later, during the Civil War (1642–51), both the Crown and the Parliamentarians asked for college plate. Some colleges complied to varying degrees, but most evaded by hiding or dispersing their plate. The extent of their success in these evasions was such that although only a limited amount of plate survives from before the Civil War, this seems to be due to the practice of replacing old plate with newly fashioned pieces rather than because it fell prey to either King or Parliament.

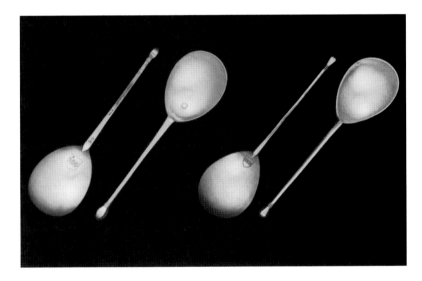

These silver spoons are not hallmarked but are engraved with the arms of Whittington and were made around AD 1400–1420. They were donated to the Worshipful Company of Mercers by Richard Whittington, Mayor of London (1397–8, 1406–7 and 1419–20).

2 Silver and Status

Silver beaker from a cemetery of 53 particularly rich graves in Marlik Tepe, Gilan province, north-west Iran. The cemetery belonged to the 'Amlash culture', one of the most distinctive Iranian cultures of the late 2nd and early 1st millennia BC. H. 13.3 cm.

The use and ownership of precious metals has long been associated with social status. This association has been considered by many societies as so fundamental that at various times throughout history sumptuary laws, defining what may be owned, worn or even eaten by whom, have been introduced to preserve social distinctions. In seventeenth-century Massachusetts, for example, more people could afford silver than the authorities thought should be allowed to flaunt it. They declared their 'utter detestation and dislike that men and women of mean condition should take upon them the garb of gentlemen by wearing gold or silver lace …' and passed a law forbidding anyone with an estate worth less than £200 to wear such lace, or gold or silver buttons. Three particular areas that demonstrate the connection between silver and social status are grave goods, domestic plate and civic regalia.

The burial rituals of many cultures have involved placing objects in the grave with the body. The meaning and nature of these objects,

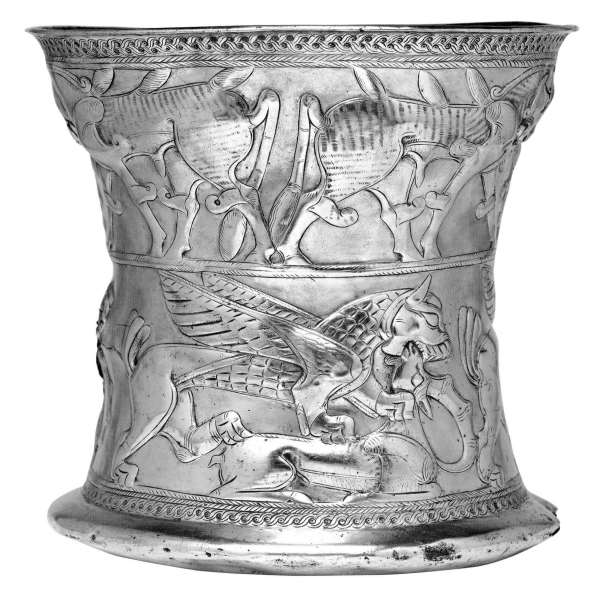

known as grave goods, are as varied as the beliefs and rituals behind them, but one of the things they can represent is the status of the grave's occupant. For example, graves at Ur, Egypt and Sutton Hoo that contain silver objects are also clearly part of enormously complex and costly burial structures.

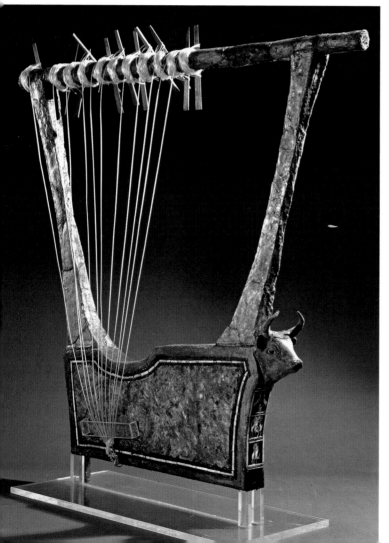

Leonard Woolley began systematically excavating the cemetery at the Ancient Mesopotamian site of Ur (in southern Iraq) in 1928. He found over 1800 graves, sixteen of which were extremely unusual. Known collectively as the Royal Graves of Ur, these graves contained sumptuous grave goods, and date to the period 2600–2400 BC. It is unclear whether these people really were royal, or perhaps religious figures, but they were buried with 74 personal attendants, and grave goods including gold and silver objects and jewellery, as well as grave furniture such as lamps, musical instruments, dishes and jars.

Ancient Egyptian burial practice was underpinned by notions of renewal and rebirth and often included providing the deceased with grave goods. These grave goods, which varied between different periods, symbolized not only the status of the person being buried but might also be expected to fulfil some function in the Afterlife, or used as offerings to the gods – particularly Osiris and Ra. Silver was clearly valued in ancient Egypt. Indeed there was a belief that the gods had silver bones. There is no native source of silver ore in Egypt, so silver was not used there until relatively late, after it had already become well established in the Middle East. Even after it became available, the use of silver seems to have varied, perhaps according to differing fashions or beliefs. The tomb of the New Kingdom king, Tutankhamun (1336–1327 BC), contained little silver, but in around 872 BC Sheshonq II, one of the 'Libyan' kings of the 22nd Dynasty, was buried in a silver coffin.

(far left) One of three wooden lyres excavated from a grave in the Royal Cemetery at Ur. It is encased in sheet silver, attached by small silver nails and has a bull's head on the front, also made of silver. The inlaid decoration is made of shell and lapis lazuli. H. 106 cm.

(above) Silver model of a Nile boat, one of two found in the tomb of Queen Ahhotep, dating to about 1295 BC. She was wife of the 17th Dynasty king, Taa.

The connection between boats and death is strong in a wide range of cultures, one of the best known perhaps being the ancient Greek and Roman myth of Charon the Underworld ferryman, who was thought to carry the recently deceased across the River Styx in his boat. The great ship burial discovered at the Anglo-Saxon cemetery site at Sutton Hoo, Suffolk, in 1939, provides a stunning example of ship

Silver bowls and spoons from the early 7th-century ship-burial at Sutton Hoo, Suffolk, England. These were all made in East Mediterranean workshops and may have come to East Anglia as a gift. Possession and use of such silver was a way of declaring wealth and status.
Diam. 22.5 cm (bowls);
L. 25.5 cm (spoons).

burial and silver being used to demonstrate status. The remains of the ship indicate it was approximately 27 metres (29 yards) long and 4.5 metres (5 yards) wide, making it longer, for example, than any of the three ships Columbus took across the Atlantic 800 years later. Given its scale, it seems that the person being commemorated was a man of importance, possibly even a king of the East Anglian dynasty. The burial contained the largest quantity of silver ever discovered in a grave including ten shallow bowls, two spoons, a great dish, a bowl with a classical head in profile, a ladle and a plain cup. Much of the silver came from the eastern Mediterranean, probably from the Byzantine empire. This level of affluence, and the ability to dispose of it in a grave, was obviously only within the grasp of a very few.

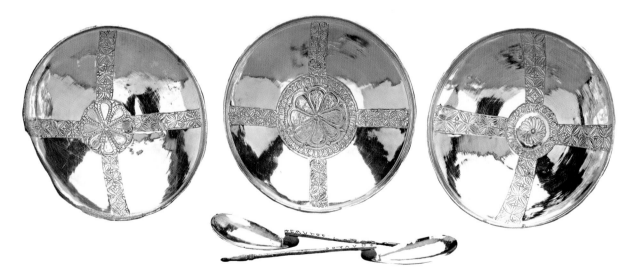

The people buried at Ur, in Egypt and at Sutton Hoo were celebrated magnificently after death and from their grave goods we can tell that they had clearly enjoyed the trappings of power and wealth during life. However, the rise of Christianity in Western Europe from the sixth century onwards changed burial rituals. From this time the inclusion of personal objects in burials diminishes, and along with it, the insight they can give us into the societies that produced them. Most of our knowledge of silver production, use and ownership in Western Europe between the sixth and the sixteenth centuries comes instead from other sources – hoards, written and physical evidence within the Church (the major patron of silver production), and other documentary evidence such as wills.

Most existing examples of British domestic silver made before the sixteenth century are spoons and drinking vessels, although a greater range survives from after this period, as ownership of domestic plate began to increase after the Reformation. Increasing personal wealth and falling silver prices meant that silver was no longer the preserve of the aristocracy, but became part of the domestic ware of gentlemen, yeomen and townspeople. To own silver was a mark of status and, importantly in those turbulent centuries, an easily convertible form of wealth. Only later did the notions of heirlooms, collector's

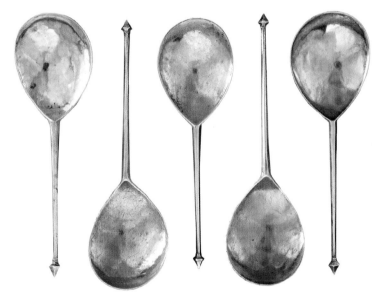

Five 14th-century spoons, found concealed in a wall of St Michael's Church, Abberley, Worcestershire. L. 14.8 cm.

Parcel gilt (partly gilt) dishes from the 'Armada Service', made in London around AD 1581–1601. The service, a unique survival of English dining silver, contains twenty-six dishes, each engraved with the arms of Sir Christopher Harris (about 1553–1625) of Radford, Devon, and his wife. Diam. 12.1 cm.

items and aesthetically pleasing objects become significant as reasons in themselves for acquiring silver.

By the mid sixteenth century, royalty, aristocracy, gentry, colleges and livery companies alike were setting great store by the conspicuous wealth and status demonstrated by silver. Tudor monarchs owned huge quantities of silver and gold, which was given and received as gifts and brought out to impress on important state occasions, an example lavishly followed by the aristocracy and gentry.

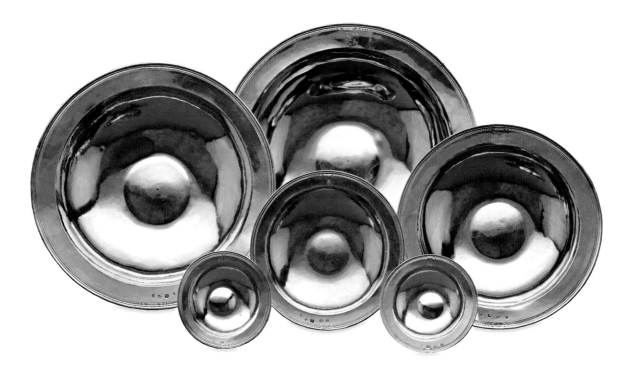

Around this time European dining customs, style and court ritual were imported from France, where the amount of silver and gold to be displayed by different ranks of society was clearly defined. The most important element in formal dining was the buffet, a sideboard where ornamental displays of silver, silver-gilt and gold dishes, bowls and platters were piled high. The taller the pile, the more honoured and impressed the guests were likely to be. At Maria de Medici's wedding in Florence in 1608, the buffet was reported to have reached the ceiling. The importance with which the Tudor aristocracy regarded the possession and display of plate as an indicator of rank and status may be judged by the fact that, at his death in 1553, the Duke of Northumberland left 10,000 ounces (283.5 kg) of silver.

This possession of silver was part of the standard by which the upper echelons of society asserted their status and judged that of their neighbours. However, as England became wealthier, people of lower rank were able to afford silver and to aspire to the status it represented. To reinforce one's status it helped to be able to display a coat of arms on the sideboard silver. Following the long-standing tradition of the aristocracy of representing their coats of arms on their possessions as evidence of their standing and lineage, engravers were much in demand to emblazon silver pieces with the arms, patron saints, or personal devices and ciphers of the upper classes and, later, for less noble clients. Designs could be reflections of status, not just marks of ownership. Presumably a combination of these reasons convinced George Booth, Earl of Warrington, to have his coronet and cipher engraved on his chamber pots.

Changes in silver manufacturing techniques during the seventeenth and eighteenth centuries further threatened the possession of silver as a mark of high status. The introduction of rolling mills some time before 1740 allowed for the rapid production of silver sheet of an even thickness. This made the production of table pieces quicker and easier,

Silver-gilt cup and cover, and sideboard dish, display pieces made by the most celebrated and successful London goldsmith of the period, Paul de Lamerie (1688–1751), in 1723. They were commissioned by the Honourable George Treby, MP (around 1684–1742), who had his arms engraved on the cup and cast and chased on to the dish. Diam. 60.8 cm (dish).

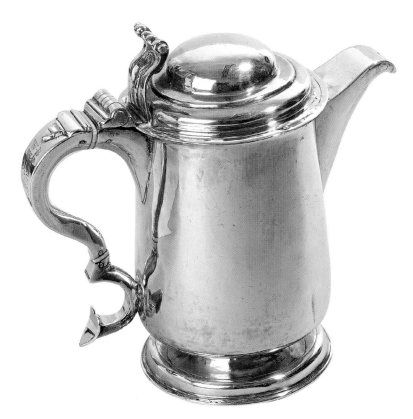

Tankard converted into a coffee-pot.

and therefore cheaper, as it was no longer necessary to hammer the silver out from ingots by hand. Another discovery, potentially even more threatening to the status of silver, was the development in 1743 of silver plate, by Thomas Boulsover of Sheffield. Copper could now be covered with silver in a way that, to the unschooled eye, made it indistinguishable from solid silver. Clearly, large shiny objects were not going to impress any longer as a sign of wealth.

The elite responded with new concepts of style and fashion. First came a new emphasis on 'table architecture'. The buffet was orchestrated in theatrical splendour by an 'architect' of the table, which became as formally designed as a garden. Symmetry was an essential features of table architecture, and involved having two of everything, which made it a little harder for those just beginning their silver collection to keep up. Another way of maintaining social distinction was to introduce new items of silver tableware to serve new foods. When tea, coffee and chocolate arrived in Britain, it became a matter of considerable status for a household to be equipped with the appropriate vessels. Indeed, it was not unknown for the owners of large beer tankards to add a curved spout and a lid to create the now far more fashionable coffee pot.

By the middle of the nineteenth century food began being presented in a series of courses, and the monumental tureens of the old table gave way to *epergnes* (elaborate dish-holders with branching arms) and then later to fruit baskets. Formal eating on a grand scale became less significant in private households, leaving colleges and livery companies among the last bastions of the traditional notions of dining and status.

In 1992 the ceremonial silver belonging to Harvard University was brought out for the inaugural dinner of the university's new president, and the university marshal explained that 'these treasured pieces of silver symbolize Harvard's continuity with its past'. Similarly the colleges of Oxford and Cambridge universities, the livery companies and other institutions such as the colleges of Physicians and Surgeons keep their own plate for special ceremonial occasions, perhaps emulating the most glittering spectacle of all – the Lord Mayor of London's annual dinner.

Most towns and cities across Britain own mayoral regalia – ceremonial items designed to signify the importance of individuals while performing their civic duties. Traditionally the regalia can include robes, a chain of office and a mayoral badge, and smaller chains for the mayor's escort and the deputy mayor. It is not unusual for swords and orbs to be part of the regalia. The only essential item however is a mace, usually made of silver.

Originally the mace was a weapon but was also adopted as a symbol of office. Many modern British officials such as the Sergeant at Arms (the monarch's bodyguard) and the Speaker of the Commons carry a mace as a symbol of their duties. The mace signifies the authority to legislate, granted to cities, towns and borough councils by the Crown, and council business can often only take place in the presence of the mace.

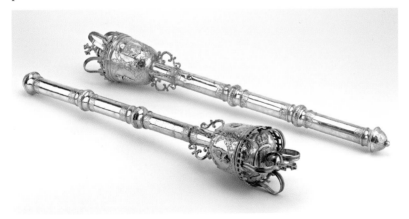

The Lifford Maces, made by David King in Dublin, Ireland, about AD 1701. The maces bear the royal arms of William III and decorative motifs include a cross, a crown, a panel, foliage, a harp, a boat, a man, a fish and an orb. They are inscribed 'BOROUGH OF LIFFORD' and 'Hugh Hamill Esq Warden 1701'. H. 83 cm.

Many accounts of how maces were acquired and what is engraved on them reflect status and civic pride. In some cases the town council paid for the mace out of civic funds, sometimes to commemorate a significant event. For example the Lifford maces from County Donegal, Ireland, reflect the victory of William III of England, Scotland and Ireland over the Jacobite forces who wanted to restore James II to the throne. In 1691 the Treaty of Limerick brought the conflict to an end and the Lifford maces, made in Dublin about 1701, bear William's arms. In Lancashire, the second civic mace of Bolton was presented by a local Justice of the Peace to commemorate 'the opening of the second Elizabethan reign, 4 September 1952', and in Surrey, the district of Surrey Heath was presented with a silver mace of 55 troy ounces (1.7 kg) in 1986 by the local office of an international corporation when one of its employees became mayor. The desire for acknowledgement of status, even reflected status, lives on.

Silver mace of the City of Sheffield.

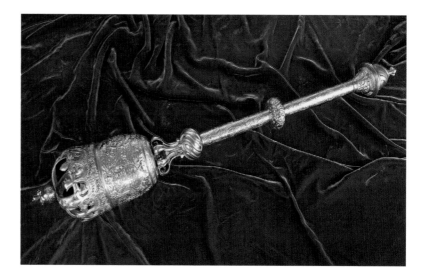

For the silversmith, though, there have to be two favourite English maces. Stafford Borough Council has four maces, including the Great Mace, which bears this proud inscription: '1655, this mace was made by Master Thomas Backhouse, ironmonger, being maior of Stafford'. To make one's own silver mace surely shows self-reliance in the extreme. Sheffield's city mace of two hundred years later provides another example of self-promotion and civic pride. The mace is of hand-beaten silver and is just over a yard long. It was presented to the city by the Duke of Norfolk to commemorate his role as the first Lord Mayor of Sheffield. Significant features include a royal crown, fleurs-de-lis, an orb and cross and the royal arms. There are also oak leaves and Yorkshire roses and, with equal significance, the arms of the Duke of Norfolk and the City of Sheffield. More discreetly inscribed is the maker's attribution: 'Omar Ramsden and Alwyn CE Carr made me in the year of our Lord 1899'.

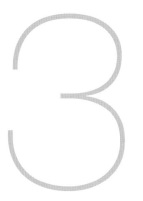

3 Adornment

Tiara made by Hunt and Roskell
in London, AD 1855.
Diam. 16.3 cm (circlet).

People wear jewellery and other personal adornments for many reasons. Some are practical: to prevent a scarf slipping or a tie flapping. Some are symbolic: to signify a particular role or membership of a group. Some, of course, are purely aesthetic: to delight in the attractiveness of jewellery. Many pieces combine several of these elements: the interplay between function and decoration is demonstrated well by a nineteenth-century gold, silver and diamond tiara. The tiara is a piece of 'convertible' jewellery, comprising three diamond-set sprays of oak leaves and acorns, which can be transformed into a brooch or a pair of comb mounts, or combined to make the striking-looking tiara.

Personal ornaments can be made from many varied materials, and many factors have affected the use of silver in different periods. Sometimes, such as in northern Europe during the early medieval period, silver took prominence due to the relative difficulty of acquiring gold. It could also be used in preference to gold for cultural

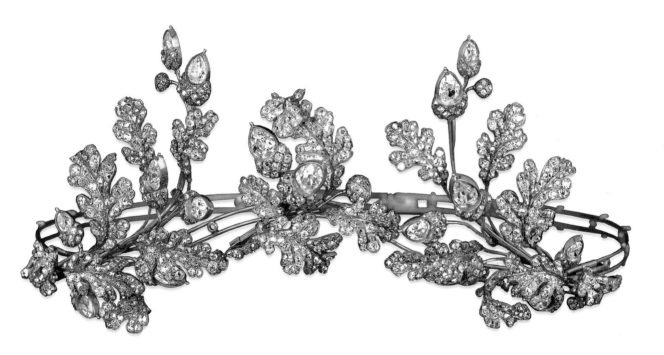

reasons, as, for example, in some parts of the Muslim world, where modesty could be offended by the flamboyance of gold. In situations such as these, niello, a black metallic alloy, was frequently used as an inlay on engraved silver to enhance its appearance.

One of the earliest pieces of silver used for adornment, dating from around 2600 BC, was excavated from the ancient Mesopotamian site of Ur. A woman's skull was discovered decorated with a headdress of gold hair ribbons and a silver comb with inlaid flowers. The universal appeal of silver hair accessories can be seen in a similar example dated centuries later and from many miles away – hair combs dating from the Chinese Liao dynasty (AD 907–1125). These silver combs are part of a long tradition in East Asia. The headdresses of both the Timorese people and the Miao people living on the borders of China, Laos, Cambodia and Tibet, for example, traditionally had silver discs attached to them.

(below) Reconstruction of a woman's headdress, from around 2600 BC, found in the Great Death Pit at Ur.

(right) Silver-gilt comb decorated with repoussé design. Royals and nobles of the 10th-century AD Liao dynasty of China were often buried with luxurious objects such as this. W. 18.2 cm.

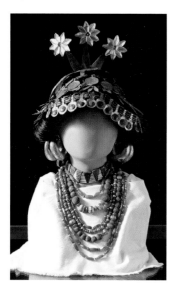

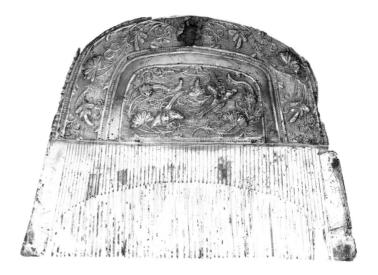

Earrings also have a long history, and in certain cultures, the range of surviving items is wide. Diadems, earrings and temporal pendants (pendants worn on the temple area of the head) appear intermittently during Roman times. Temporal pendants appear again in thirteenth-century Russia, as do *ryasnas* (decorations hanging from diadems or headdresses). There are other examples from Anglo-Saxon and Viking finds in the seventh century, and from Indonesia in the seventeenth century.

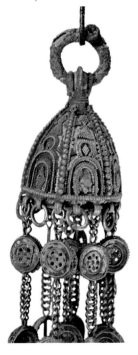

(left) 12th-century AD silver temporal pendant, one of a pair found in a hoard in Kiev, Ukraine. It would have been worn suspended from a crown or head-dress. The pendant is decorated with an interlaced, mythical animal and geometric designs on a black, nielloed ground. Diam. 5.2 cm.

(below) A *ryasna* – part of a Russian headdress from the 13th century.

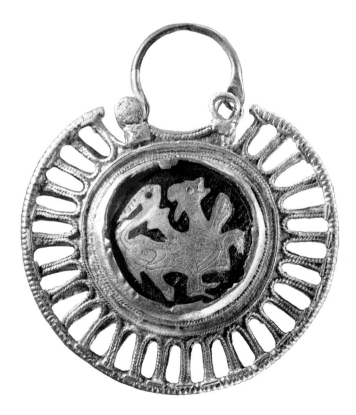

Sumptuary laws, forbidding especially the adornments worn by women, were known in the Roman Republic during the third and second centuries BC. However, as the wealth flowing into Rome grew with its empire, so did the desire for lavish display amongst its women. The emperor Caligula's wife, Lollia Polina, may have set a trend, as she reportedly appeared wearing jewellery on her head, neck, arms and hands as a matter of course. There are extensive examples of a wide variety of necklaces, chokers and pendants from across the Roman empire, although more splendid examples survive in gold than in silver.

Silver pendant from a jeweller's hoard, buried in Snettisham, Norfolk, about AD 155. L. 2.3 cm.

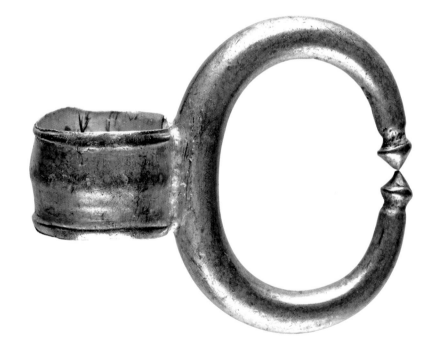

One of the most impressive neck decorations is the torc, ring-shaped necklets made of a open circle of metal, often with large decorative terminals at each end. The Romans associated this form with the peoples of northern Europe, where it seems to have been a symbol of status. A magnificent silver torc dating from the first century BC was unearthed at Snettisham in Norfolk (see Chapter 1), while a Merovingian one containing rock crystal survives from the fifth century AD.

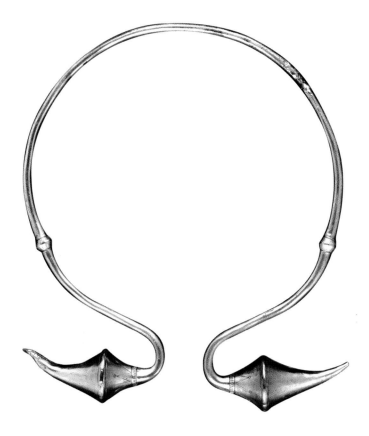

An impressive torc found in a silver hoard known as the Córdoba Treasure, buried about 100 BC in the Molino de Marrubial (modern Córdoba), Spain. It was hidden just after Spain had been conquered by the Romans. Diam. 16 cm.

Examples of neck jewellery from later periods include a complex necklace of strung beads and silver from a ninth-century Viking grave excavated at Birka, Sweden, and a silver pendant, dating from the tenth or eleventh century, from the Aska burial site in Sweden. In modern times necklaces are known to have been designed to embody significance. For example in 1912, Bernard Cuzner made a suffragette necklace, echoing the colours of the suffragette movement by setting green chalcedony, white aquamarines and pink-mauve sapphires in silver gilt.

Silver pendant from a Viking burial at Aska, Sweden, depicting a woman, probably the Norse goddess Freja.

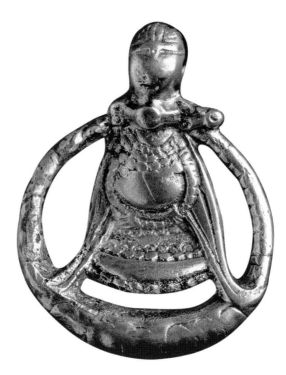

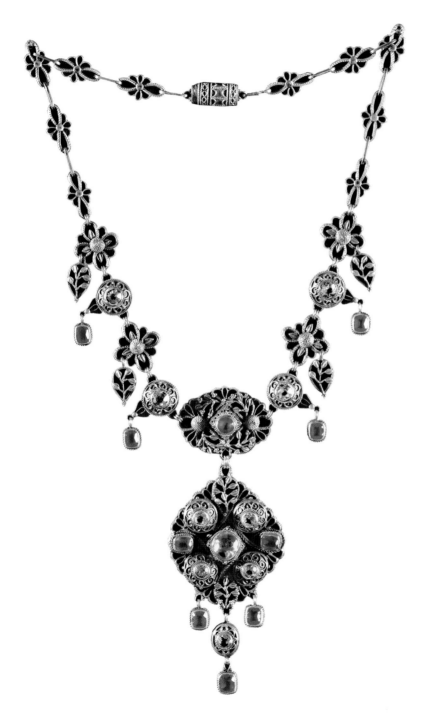

Bernard Cuzner's suffragette necklace in chalcedony, aquamarine and pink-mauve sapphire; 19th century, Birmingham.

Archaeologists classify ancient brooches according to their form, using a bewildering range of different names. One pair, found in Chorley, Lancashire, and probably dating from the second century AD, are of the type known as 'trumpet brooches'. This design may have been a Roman fashion introduced to Britain, and examples have been found in copper, silver and silver gilt. They were designed to be worn together, with a fastening between to hold a cloak, tunic, or similar piece of clothing in place. The forms of brooches changed with fashion. Radiate-headed brooches were used by the Lombards in the sixth century, square-headed brooches appear in Anglo-Saxon finds, pin brooches are first associated with Ireland and then the Vikings, while quatrefoil designs were popular amongst the Merovingians.

Silver Romano-British trumpet fibula set, 2nd century AD, from Chorley, Lancashire.

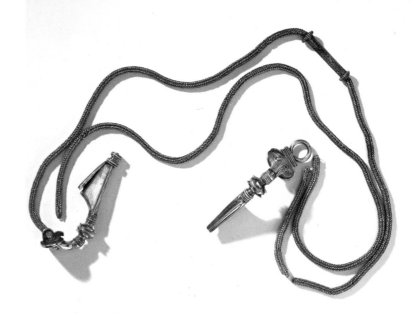

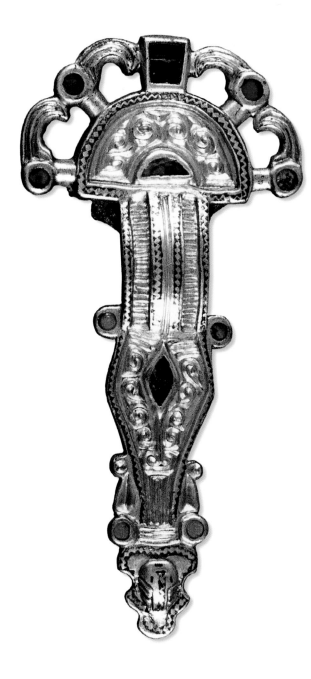

Gilded silver radiate brooch said to be from the 6th-century cemetery at Herpes, Charente, France. Brooches like this would have been worn by women from northern France, the Rhineland and southern Germany to Italy, perhaps as a sign of rank. Regional variations are distinguished by the shape of the foot-plate and the number of knobs round the radiate head. L. 10.1 cm.

There are numerous examples of decorative brooches, pins, buckles and belts made by the Celts, Anglo-Saxons, Merovingians and Vikings of northern Europe. From the ninth century AD an impressive amount of bullion, mostly silver, was taken by Vikings from many European towns, while in England a payment known as the Danegeld was made to them to prevent them encroaching from the lands they controlled in the north and east (the Danelaw). Some sources suggest six tons was taken from Paris in AD 845, and more than three tons from England in AD 991. To this must be added a greater amount acquired in trade. It is not surprising that some of this large quantity of silver in circulation should be transformed into jewellery.

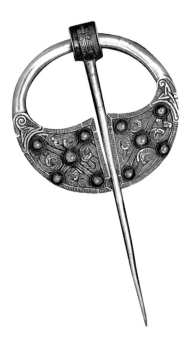

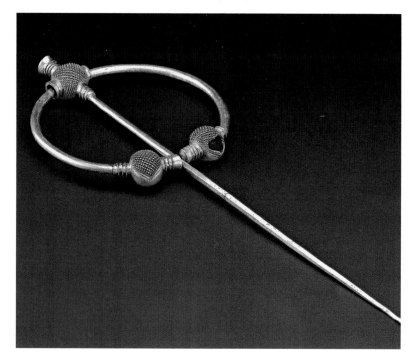

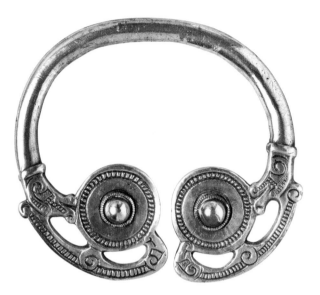

Silver bossed penannular Viking
brooch from the Goldsborough
hoard dating from the 9th–10th
centuries AD. The brooch, which
has lost its pin, has animal heads
joined to bossed terminals and
openwork animals extending
around each end. Diam. 8.5 cm.

Pins and brooches that have survived from the fifth to the eighth centuries all consist of a strong pin, sometimes made of iron, with a silver head. These heads have a variety of shapes and are decorated in a number of different fashions. A Pictish pin from the fifth century has a small round head set at an angle, decorated with a typical Celtic design. A sixth-century silver-gilt pin found in Lincolnshire draws on the Scandinavian tradition for its decoration, with animal motifs rather than abstract shapes.

(left) Disc-headed Irish or
Pictish silver pin dating from the
5th–6th century AD and
decorated with typical back-to-
back 'C' scrolls. L. 32.8 cm.

(far left) Silver-gilt dress pin from
the Anglo-Saxon cemetery at
Sleaford, Lincolnshire, England.
The long curved shaft of this
large and unusual pin is typical of
Anglian culture areas in eastern
England. It is decorated with
stylized animals that are similar
to the decorative elements on
the helmet from the ship-burial
at Sutton Hoo. L. 15.4 cm.

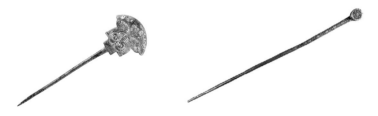

One design, the penannular brooch, has been popular at many periods in Europe. This is a circular cloak pin with a break in the ring so that the pin can pass through and be twisted to lock it. An early and splendid example is the Londesborough brooch from eighth-century Ireland. Perhaps the most magnificent surviving example of a brooch, however, is the Fuller brooch, dating from the ninth century. The skill and artistry involved in its production demonstrates the development of Anglo-Saxon silversmithing skills. It is hammered rather than cast, and extraordinarily finely worked with a design depicting the Five Senses. It is so remarkably well preserved that it was once assumed to be a fake.

8th–9th century AD silver and gold penannular brooch from Ireland known as the Londesborough Brooch. The brooch is a heavy silver ring cast with complex patterns of interlace, spirals, animal and bird motifs and then thickly gilded on the front. L. 24 cm (pin).

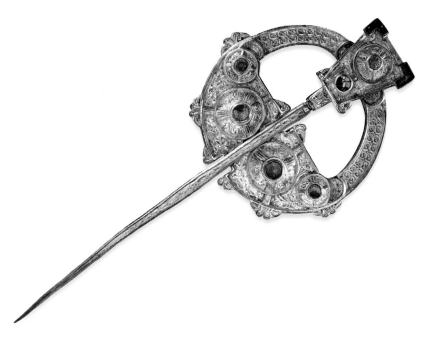

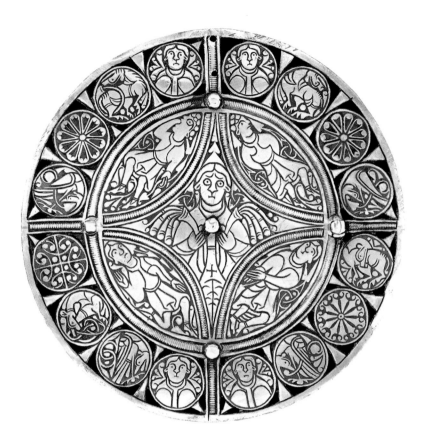

The Anglo-Saxon silver disc brooch known as the Fuller Brooch bears a finely worked representation of the Five Senses, inlaid with niello. Diam. 11.4 cm.

Like brooches, belts are functional objects that often became highly decorative items of adornment. Wearing a belt often carries social significance – it might show that the wearer can afford to carry a weapon, as in fifteenth-century Italy, for example, or to denote an activity associated with status, such as riding a horse in the Eastern Zhou period in China (770–221 BC).

Mid-7th century Anglo-Saxon belt buckle from Crundale Down, Kent, England. Although the triangle shape of the belt is typically Anglo-Saxon, the decorative motif of a fish is usually associated with early Christianity. L. 15.3 cm.

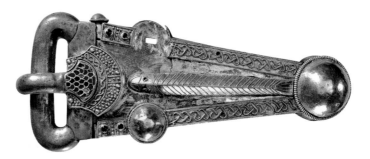

7th-century Merovingian iron and silver buckle from Amiens, Somme, France. It is very elaborately decorated with interlaced Scandinavian-style animals and animal heads, indicating the owner's high social status. L. 31.1 cm.

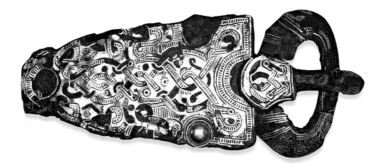

15th-century Venetian belt fitting, decorated with niello.

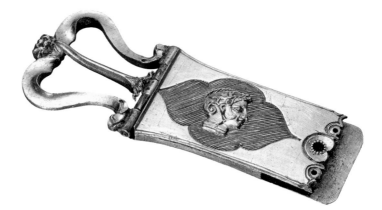

How a belt is decorated can also reveal religious and cultural associations. For example, a seventh-century silver and gold Anglo-Saxon belt buckle found in Kent is decorated with a fish, which is a Christian symbol, while further south, in the Somme, at about the same time, a woman was wearing a silver and iron buckle of similar shape but decorated with animal heads, after the (pagan) Scandinavian style. A thirteenth-century Turkish belt sports a number of finely tooled silver gilt panels as well as a buckle and loops for hanging a dagger, while a set of fifteenth-century Venetian belt fittings is decorated with fine niello work.

Unlike buckles, brooches and pins, which have to be worn attached to clothing, bracelets and finger-rings offer an opportunity for pure decoration. They can draw the eye towards a slender wrist, a youthful arm or a muscular bicep, a fact as apparent to the Egyptians, Greeks, Romans, Vikings and Slavs as it is to us today. Bracelets have been found among grave goods buried over 1500 years ago, and Viking hoards contain many examples of armlets worn by both men and women.

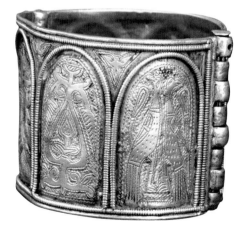

Hammered silver sheet bracelet from a hoard found in Kiev, Ukraine, and probably buried at the time of the Tartar invasions and sack of Kiev around AD 1240. The heraldic bird motifs are a popular motif in early Slav art, and are thought to be symbols of the ruling dynasty in Kiev. Diam. 6.9 cm.

Finger-rings must be the most universally worn item of jewellery, though relatively few fine historical examples survive in silver outside the northern European and Islamic areas. Rings embody a great complexity of symbolism: they can signify commitment and fidelity (such as engagement and wedding rings); membership of a particular group (such as a class ring from an American university); or status and power (such as the ring worn by the pope). Even when there is no particular significance, there is a long tradition of wearing rings just for decoration.

As bracelets draw attention to the arms and wrists, so anklets – whether the fine chains currently popular in Europe or the more substantial ones typical of certain styles of Arab and Indian jewellery – emphasize a well-turned ankle. Similarly finger rings are paralleled by toe rings which are particularly popular in India. In some cultures, such as ancient Egypt, toe rings appear regularly, but in far fewer numbers than other sorts of jewellery. This has led to speculation as to whether their limited occurrence denotes the special status of the wearer, perhaps as a soothsayer.

Silversmiths have produced such a multitude of items that it is not always clear to what extent they worked to meet demand or to stimulate it. An influential smith may certainly be in a position to foster fashion, especially in more recent times when, at least in the West, silversmithing has become regarded as more closely allied to art than to craft. After the American War of Independence, the silversmith Paul Revere broadened his business with the production of knee buckles that secured loose knee-length trousers. Functional reasons did not require that they be made of silver, but they also emphasized the calf, and therefore the more elegant the metal, the better the effect. Fashions, however, do not always change to suit the smith. Buckles were popular for many centuries and, as with buckles on clothing, those on shoes became far more ornate than practicality demanded. They were frequently detachable so that they outlasted the shoes they originally adorned. As fashion accessories, however, their popularity declined in the 1790s with Harvey Kennedy's patenting and popularization of the shoelace.

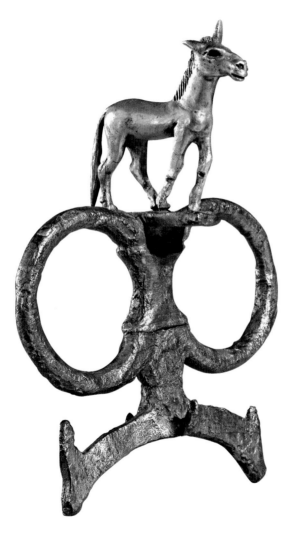

Gold and silver rein ring found among the bones of two oxen lying in front of the remains of a sledge in the 'Queen's Grave', Ur, southern Iraq, dating to about 2600–2400 BC. Fixed to the top of the rings is a donkey or wild ass made of cast electrum. H. 13.5 cm.

More recently individual smiths have become known by name and are therefore themselves becoming part of the world of fashion. We know that the diamond oak leaf tiara was made in London by Hunt & Roskell in 1855, not least because both Anne Hull Grundy, who purchased it in 1970, and its original owner(s) made sure that it remained in the box in which it had arrived, with the prestigious and fashionable maker's name clearly shown. Today, one assumes that few Georg Jensen boxes are discarded.

The tradition of ornamenting portable objects or attachments and fittings predates any efforts on the part of smiths to increase their business. Grave goods from Ur, dating from between 2600–2400 BC, include a silver and gold rein ring, found among the bones of the oxen buried with the grave's inhabitant. Later warriors adorned their horses' harnesses with silver, often apparently to complement the silver weaponry they carried. Examples include a silver saddle decoration

7th-century AD Sasanian sword scabbard, said to come from Dailaman, north-west Iran, made of wood covered with silver sheets. The scabbard would have been worn in an oblique position, suspended from the belt by two straps running through loops riveted on the back of two 'P-shaped' attachments. L. 92 cm.

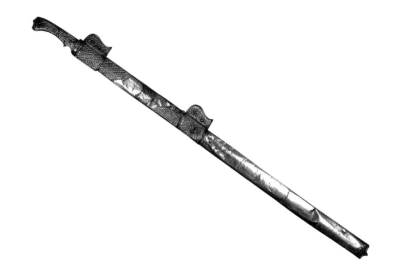

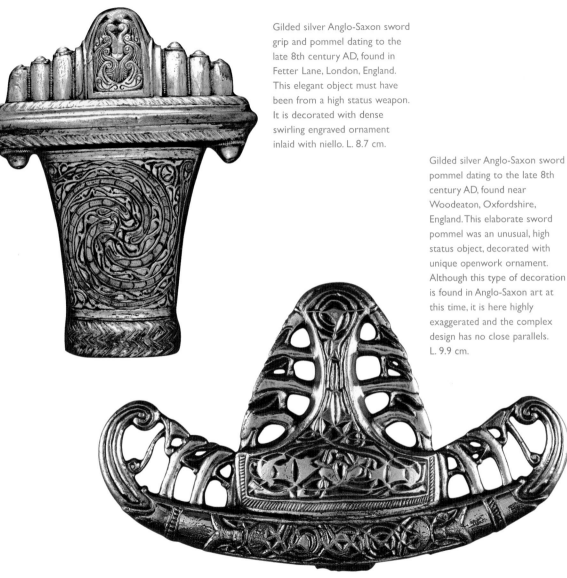

Gilded silver Anglo-Saxon sword grip and pommel dating to the late 8th century AD, found in Fetter Lane, London, England. This elegant object must have been from a high status weapon. It is decorated with dense swirling engraved ornament inlaid with niello. L. 8.7 cm.

Gilded silver Anglo-Saxon sword pommel dating to the late 8th century AD, found near Woodeaton, Oxfordshire, England. This elaborate sword pommel was an unusual, high status object, decorated with unique openwork ornament. Although this type of decoration is found in Anglo-Saxon art at this time, it is here highly exaggerated and the complex design has no close parallels. L. 9.9 cm.

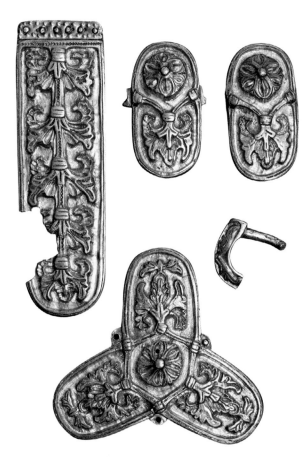

Silver mounts from a Frankish baldric: highly decorative, but without function.

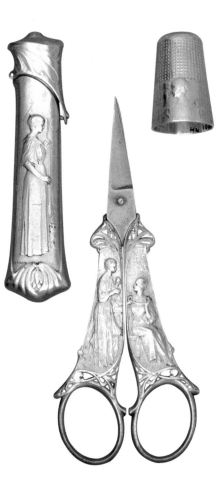

Silver-gilt nécessaire of needle-case, scissors and thimble. Made in France by Julien Duval, 1900–1912. H. 9.9 cm (thimble).

from fifth-century Japan and a silver scabbard from seventh-century Iran and two exceptionally unusual eighth-century Anglo-Saxon silver sword pommels have been found in England. From the ninth century a Viking spearhead decorated with silver survives, as do the silver mounts for a Frankish baldric (belt worn over the shoulder) and bridle bits from Russia. In the thirteenth century Japanese warriors carried swords and used stirrups that involved the use of *shakudō* (a copper and gold alloy), decorated with gold and silver.

The modern-day Western understanding of accessories, especially silver ones, began with the late Victorians and was reinforced by the Art Nouveau and Art Deco movements. In Victorian times silver accessories became available even to those earning a modest wage, rather than solely royalty and the nobility. Silver was used to create or embellish many personal items such as walking sticks, snuff boxes, cigarette cases and sovereign cases for men, and, for women, silver chatelaines (belt hooks or clasps with chains attached for keys, scissors and other household necessities), fans, handbags, patch boxes and card cases to name but a few. None of these items needs to be made of silver – but they often are.

The current plethora of modern accessories, from vanity cases, cigarette holders, evening bags and lipstick cases to pet collars and mobile phone covers, results at least in part from the Western preoccupation with personal expression, in which personal adornment plays such an important part, and which increased wealth allows.

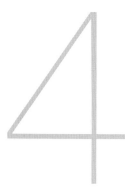

Silversmiths

Smiths have been represented in myths and legends from around the world, though they have always had a rather mixed press. Although they were credited with immense and often magical powers, they were sometimes depicted as giants or dwarfs, and in the case of the one-eyed Cyclops, their physical peculiarities were even more pronounced. For example Hephaestus, the Greek god of blacksmiths, craftsmen, artisans, sculptors, metals and fire, is usually portrayed as lame, ugly, misshapen and walking with a stick. He was himself a skilled smith and produced many of the powerful magical objects owned by the Olympian gods: Hermes' winged helmets and sandals, Eros' bows and arrows, and Aphrodite's girdles. Three Cyclops worked for Hephaestus in his workshops on Mount Olympus, where they were responsible for the creation of thunder, lightning and thunderbolts.

The Romans associated Vulcan, their god of fire and volcanoes, with Hephaestus, and considered him responsible for the manufacture of Jupiter's thunderbolts, and of arms and armour that rendered its

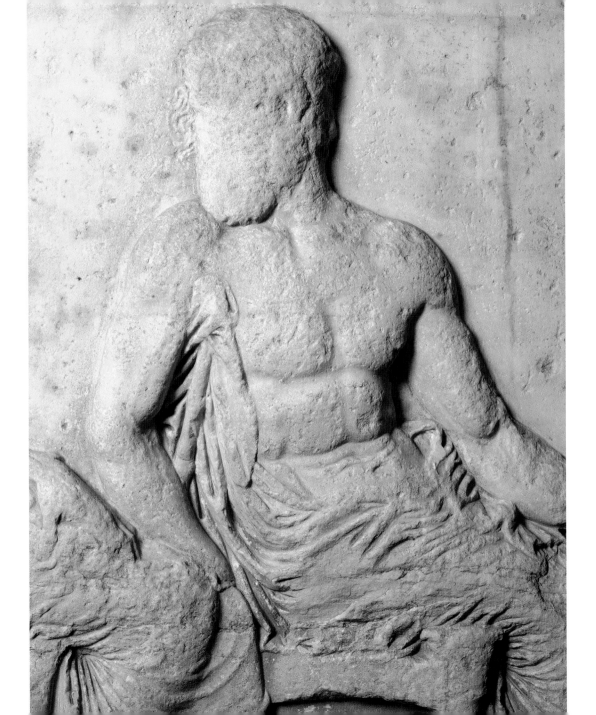

wearer almost invincible. Perhaps oddly, he was also the god of art. Like Hephaestus, Vulcan was depicted as small, ugly and lame.

Silver-gilt tazza (footed bowl) made in Augsburg, Germany, about AD 1575–1600, with a central scene in relief showing Vulcan's Forge. The decoration was made by raising the surface of the silver from the reverse (embossing), after which the surface was worked on the front (chasing). Diam. 20 cm (bowl).

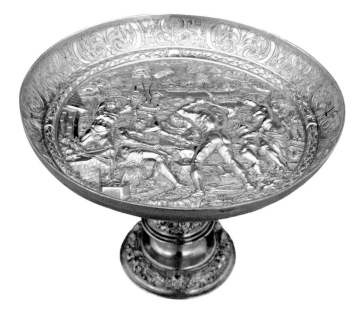

The smiths of early medieval Norse and Celtic legend are perhaps less grandiose than the Olympians, although they were also responsible for the production of weapons of almost magical power. Dwarf smiths in Norse sagas wrought magic swords and Thor's hammer, and the Celtic smith Goibhniu appears as a skilful worker who makes spears and swords for heroic warriors (although at least some of his time is also spent receiving the admiration of young and marriageable women).

Another characteristic of mythical smiths is that they can be vengeful when thwarted or cheated and their skill can easily turn to cunning. In one Norse saga, Weland the Smith was taken prisoner by King Nidud, hamstrung, and held on an island where he was forced to make jewellery. His response was to kill the king's sons, make goblets from their skulls and present their mother with jewellery made from their teeth and eyes. For good measure he seduced the king's daughter and then escaped using wings he had created for himself.

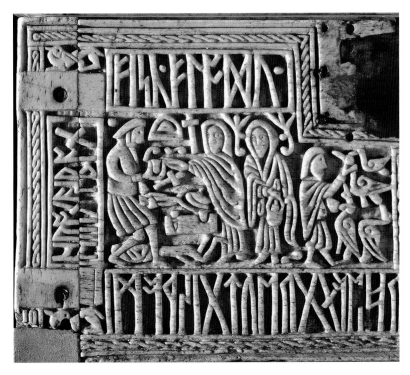

Detail from the Anglo-Saxon carved whalebone casket known as the Franks Casket, made in Northumbria, England, in the first half of the 8th century AD. This scene depicts episodes from the legend of Weland the Smith, who is shown at his forge on the left. H. 10.9 cm.

Even in more modern times, five centuries after the legend of Weland, the Tuareg people of North Africa said of their silversmiths that they were 'older than memory, proud as the crow and mischievous in mind'. In short, silversmiths seem to be regarded as an interesting but not altogether attractive group of people. We might ask ourselves whether real-life silversmiths are as impressive – or as shady – as their legendary counterparts and whether they have lived up to the reputation smiths seem to have acquired so early in history. A brief look at the way gold and silver workers fit into society and how they have related to their patrons may provide clues as to how this reputation arose.

The distinction between smithing and other activity has not always been clearly delineated. Those who worked with silver might be specialist silversmiths but could also be jewellers, goldsmiths, or metal workers. In medieval England everyone who worked in precious metals were known simply as goldsmiths, whereas nowadays everyone who works with silver is referred to as a silversmith. Sources from various parts of the Islamic world refer to a wide range of professionals who worked with silver: silversmiths, coin makers, jewellers, specialist engravers, and those responsible for smelting.

Detail from a brass pen box exquisitely inlaid in gold and silver, made in Iran in AD 1281. This is the maker's signature, positioned under the clasp of the pen box so as to remain hidden when the box was closed. H. 3.1 cm (box).

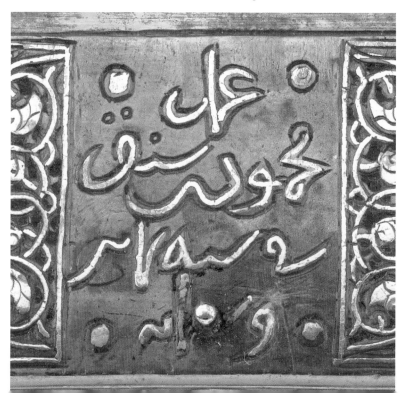

Although craftsmen tend to gravitate towards urban areas, where patronage is more available, they are often drawn from minority or outsider groups rather than from the local population. For example, there was a long tradition of Jewish craftspeople in both Oman and Syria, and many Huguenot silversmiths arrived in London from continental Europe from the mid seventeenth century onwards. This is usually a voluntary migration, towards the sources of raw materials and patronage and away from religious or political oppression, but on occasion it was an enforced removal. In Peru in the eleventh to fifteenth centuries, for example, the Chimú people were renowned as skilled goldsmiths and silversmiths. When the Inca conquered the Chimú in 1470, they took large numbers of Chimú smiths to their capital Cusco and other provincial capitals.

Silversmiths occasionally emerge as members of close-knit groups, sharing not only the secrets of their trade but often close family ties, shared beliefs, customs and even languages that are not necessarily understood by the community in which they are working. They provide a service for which they are valued, but in other ways they may be outsiders and therefore potentially suspect. It is perhaps partly for this reason that they began to organize themselves to exercise control over their trade: to increase public confidence, protect their position and facilitate their integration.

Hoard from Snettisham, Norfolk, containing scrap silver, ingots, a few pieces of scrap gold and a quartz burnishing tool. It represents part of the stock of a jeweller working in the area in around AD 155. Though it has no direct connection with the great Iron Age hoards found at Snettisham, it may be evidence of a long tradition of gold- and silver-working in the area.
H. 17.5 cm (pot).

Guaranteeing the purity of the silver used was an issue of primary importance. Pure silver is too soft for most practical purposes so it is alloyed with other metals, usually copper, and this gave rise to attempts to impose standards. Probably the oldest standard still in use today is sterling silver, consisting of silver and copper in the fixed ratio of 92.5 per cent silver to 7.5 per cent copper. When this standard originated is unclear, though it was being used by the twelfth and thirteenth centuries in Europe.

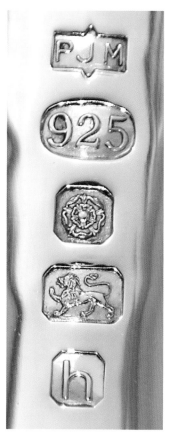

Hallmark showing (top to bottom) the sponsor's mark, the standard of silver, two marks referring to the assay office which tested the item, and the date letter indicating the year the piece was assayed and thus the assay master responsible.

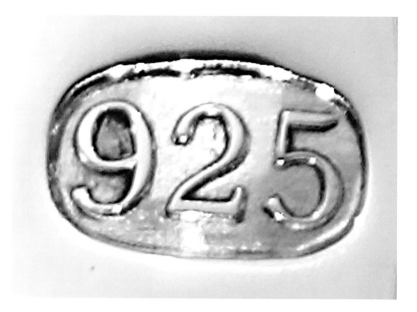

Another way of creating professional standards was the creation of guilds. By the fourteenth century in Britain, as in many other European countries, guilds were becoming increasingly prominent. The Worshipful Company of Goldsmiths in London exerted strict control over its members. Personal and professional behaviour was regulated, together with the purity of the metal used and the quality of the workmanship. Full membership of the Guild was only achieved after a lengthy apprenticeship and the production of a masterpiece, but to be a member brought status and, usually, prosperity.

Although these standards were apparently adopted to provide protection for the public, it was clear that they could also be used to protect the Company's own interests. To become an apprentice involved influence, personal contact, or existing goodwill, as did acquiring the materials to produce a masterpiece. The Company was also responsible for the application of the hallmark to a piece of work (a right granted in AD 1300 by Edward I) guaranteeing its quality – without which it could not be sold. New smiths arriving in London found themselves restricted by the established local smiths, as the Company often refused, or attempted to refuse, admittance to foreigners, or harassed them in their business. This problem was particularly acute at the end of the seventeenth century, when many highly skilled Huguenot silversmiths sought refuge in England.

This tension between the maintenance of standards and the imposition of restrictive practices has still not been resolved, and continues to concern international bodies such as the European Union. While in the UK there is a requirement for all white metal to be hallmarked before it can be sold as silver, various other countries with particular interests dispute whether this constitutes protection for the public or the restriction of free trade.

Despite membership of a guild, not all smiths behaved in as creditable a manner as was perhaps expected of them. For example the famous Renaissance figure Benvenuto Cellini (1500–71), was a goldsmith, sculptor, flautist, and criminal. As an apprenticed goldsmith he was banished from Florence for brawling while still a teenager. Later, as a talented coin and medal maker, he gravitated towards the wealthy patrons of Rome, where he undertook

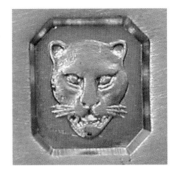

(above) Leopard's head hallmark, first adopted in 1300 when it was specified in the statue setting out silver standards. At first it was used across England, although much later it was considered to signify only London-assayed silver.

(opposite) Silver standard punch mark.

Portrait of Benvenuto Cellini by
Raphael Morghen, after Giorgio
Vasari, AD 1822. This is taken
from Vasari's tondo of Cosimo
de' Medici among his architects
and engineers in the Palazzo
Vecchio in Florence. H. 16 cm.

commissions for Pope Clement VII. Cellini seemed to settle down and adopt the sober and industrious life his guild required of him, but a murder charge and the wounding of a notary meant that once again he had to beat a hasty retreat, this time to Naples. Remarkably his talent saved him and within a year he was back in Rome, working for Pope Paul III. It was not long, however, before he fell out with the Pope's illegitimate son and fled to Florence and Venice. After a year or two Cellini was back in Rome and working once again for Paul III. Interestingly what led to his final banishment was not murder, assault or affray, but the charge (probably false) of the theft of gems from the tiara of his patron. Cellini's craft once again acted as a passport, this time to Paris, where he executed perhaps his most famous works. At the end of his career he returned to Florence and wrote an autobiography detailing the remarkable freedom his craft afforded him and the protection offered by the patrons whose status he had enhanced through his work.

In contrast to Cellini, another famous smith and 'Renaissance man', Paul Revere (1734–1818), spent his efforts in the pursuit of liberty and equality for his community. Revere learnt his trade in his father's workshop in Boston and turned his hand not only to silversmithing, but to designing, engraving, printing, and even a little dentistry. He also became active in politics, a Revolutionary soldier, and a prominent member of the Congregational Church. He played an important role in the American War of Independence (1775–83) and is famous for his 'Midnight Ride', when he brought vital information about British troop movements to Revolutionary forces at Lexington, later immortalised in a poem. As a silversmith Revere found himself making items that typified colonial standards and social stability, while he himself held views that were nothing less than treasonable. During 1768 the well-established artist John Singleton Copley painted Revere's portrait as a solid and prosperous burgher, even as he was illicitly

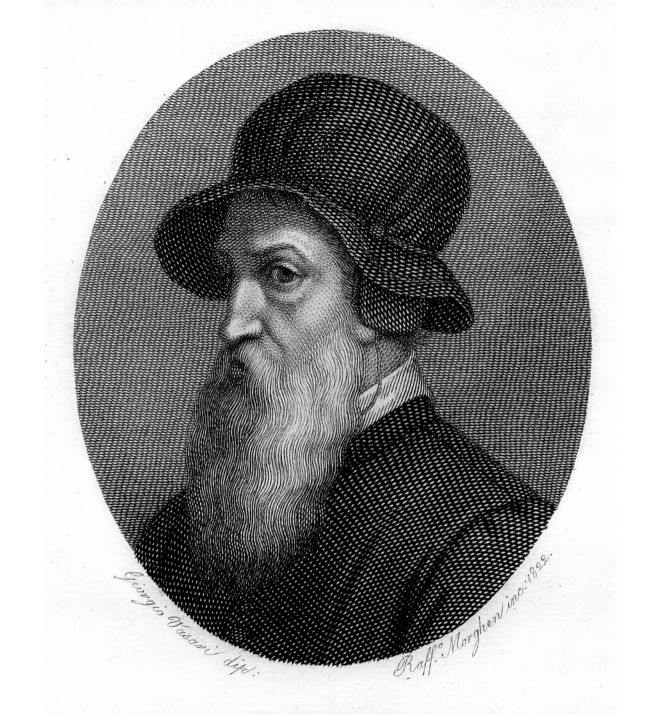

Giorgio Vasari dipt.

Raff.° Morghen inci. 1822.

making the Sons of Liberty Bowl. This bowl was engraved with the names of ninety-two members of the Sons of Liberty Society, an organization which opposed British taxation of the electorally unrepresented. Had the bowl been discovered and its authorship established, Revere would have been in serious difficulties.

Portrait of Paul Revere by John Singleton Copley, AD 1768.

(opposite) Silver bowl engraved with the names of the members of the Sons of Liberty Society, made and engraved by Paul Revere in Boston, AD 1768.

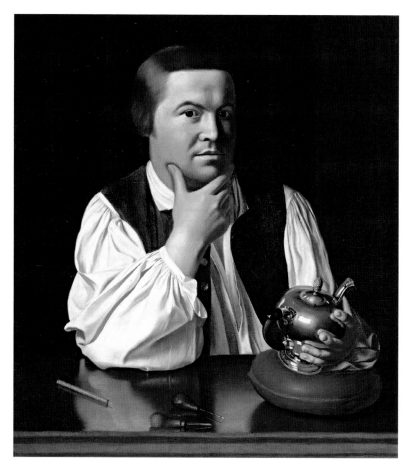

Vernon, Dan.ˡ Parker. John Marſton. Ichabod Jones. John Homer

To the Memory of the glorious NINETY-TWO: Members
of the Honᵇˡᵉ Houſe of Repreſentatives of the Maſſachuſetts-Bay;
who, undaunted by the inſolent Menaces of Villains in Power,
from a ſtrict Regard to Conſcience, and the LIBERTIES
of their Conſtituents, on the 30ᵗʰ of June 1768,

Voted   NOT TO RESCIND.

Louisa Courtauld

Unlike Cellini, Revere did not rely exclusively on wealthy patronage or protection. His account books indicate that during the course of a long career he supplied over 750 customers with a variety of small items, from buckles and buttons to spoons, mugs and tableware. His workshops expanded into copper and iron production, and he proved adept at spotting new markets, such as the demand for cast bronze bells. Both as a revolutionary and button maker, he was clearly a fascinating character.

In London at about the same time, another unusual smith was amassing a fortune. Louisa Courtauld (1729–1807) was an outsider both as a Huguenot, and as one of a relatively small group of female silversmiths. She married into the Courtaulds, a long-established family of Huguenot silversmiths, in 1749. From this time she would have helped her husband manage the workshops, not as a smith but as an employer and retailer. It would be her responsibility to find quality chasers, modellers and engravers, and to solicit and receive commissions from clients. After her husband's death in 1765 Louisa inherited the highly successful business and later took on a partner, George Cowles, formerly an apprentice of her husband, until her son was old enough to take on business responsibilities. Louisa was not a maker; some of the pieces stamped with her mark would either have been made by subcontractors for her, or they would have been bought in, already marked, and overstamped with her mark. This was a common practice among well-known retailers once they began to deal with the increasing volume of business created by the growing wealth and changing tastes of their customers. Courtauld's ability to move with these changing tastes played a part in the growing success of the firm.

Although Louisa was not a maker, women did work as artisans. They were chain makers, button makers, burnishers, finishers and polishers. Other outworkers would concentrate on casting handles or spouts, while others would engrave. All this effort and skill was

Self-portrait by Louisa Courtauld in graphite and brown chalk on paper, about AD 1800. H. 20.8 cm.

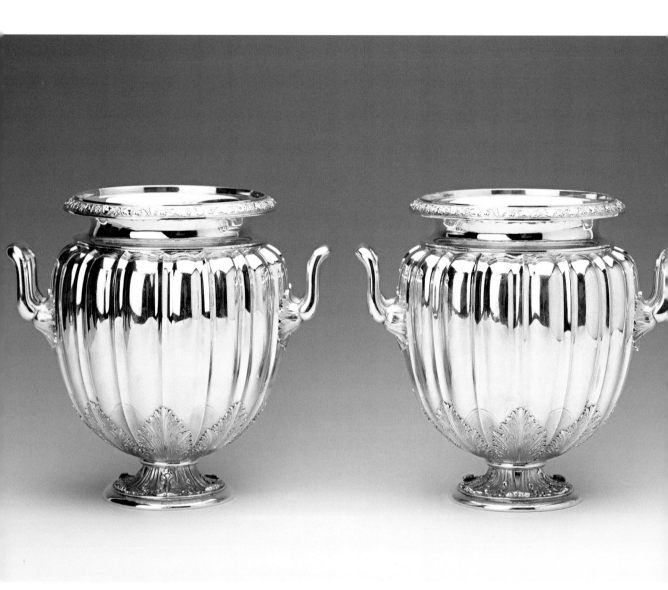

coordinated by Louisa, who would be watching out for the best work at the cheapest rates.

Throughout the eighteenth century the growth of industrialization and the wealth it produced was reflected in the growth of the silver trade. Craft workshops were no longer able to meet the demand in-house and began to make use of a whole infrastructure of subcontractors and outworkers that sprang up with increasing division of labour. At a time of expanding markets and rapidly changing tastes, silver was big business and firms grew and altered according to circumstances. By the mid eighteenth century there was a clear split within the silver business in western Europe. Some firms supplied smaller pieces to the popular market while others concentrated on magnificent pieces for the wealthier end of the market.

The story of Rundell, Bridge & Rundell illustrates the latter strategy. A small company founded in 1750 had, by 1797, evolved into a firm holding the prominent position of Royal Goldsmiths, Silversmiths, Jewellers and Medallists. One of their employees described how John Bridge 'possessed as much Pride as any Person need have, yet to anyone and to everyone by whom he expected to gain anything he was apparently the most humble and obedient Person that could well be imagined, his back was exceedingly flexible and no man in London could bow lower or oftener than could Mr Bridge'. Obsequiousness alone was not, however, enough to propel a company to the top and Rundell, Bridge & Rundell offered products that were of high quality, modern and fashionable. This was made possible because John Bridge managed to secure the services of major talents such as Thomas Hodges Baily, whose most famous work is undoubtedly his statue of Admiral Lord Nelson in London's Trafalgar Square, and Paul Storr, a talented silversmith who had already made a reputation for himself by the time he joined the company.

Pair of silver George IV wine coolers, by John Bridge.

Paul Storr was a prolific worker who maintained his own workshop and mark while also producing items for Rundells'. At the height of his time with them, he was under contract to produce 10,000 ounces (283 kg) of silverware a year. Even allowing for the large scale of many of his pieces this was a huge output. After he parted company with Rundells' they continued from strength to strength, courting patronage and relying on a network of skilled workers, while Storr took on new partners of his own. Despite his reputation his business never regained its former vigour, and after a quarrel with his latest partner and financial backer, he retired.

Perhaps it is unreasonable to view all silversmiths in comparison with a few high-profile examples such as Cellini, Revere, Courtauld and Storr. However the stories of the more flamboyant characters throw some light on how silversmiths are viewed, and perhaps something about the way they see themselves. These stories may not be the stuff of heroic myth and legend but they illustrate the reality, not the fantasy, of a smith's career. While not in possession of magical powers nor the ability to bestow invincibility on their clients, these smiths gained status and success through a combination of skill and networking. Creativity allied with business acumen rather than the patronage of the gods brings riches and reputation to modern smiths.

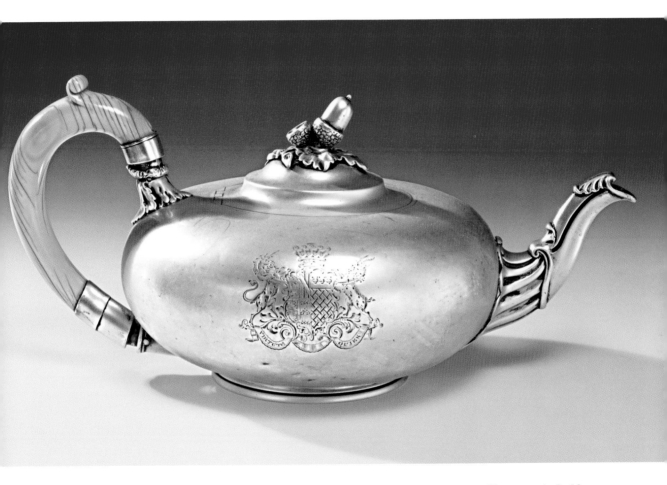

Silver teapot by Paul Storr.

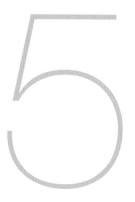

Symbolic Value

Many cultures have connected precious metals with deities, magical properties, and the stars and planets. For example, a Mayan legend from Mesoamerica refers to gold as the sweat of the sun and silver as the tears of the moon. The ancient Egyptians associated gold and silver not only with the sun and moon, and their cyclical and eternal movement, but also with the gods. Silver has frequently been used to make amulets, talismans, charms and gifts that bestow luck upon the wearer or owner, such as the silver Christening spoon traditionally given to an infant. It is, of course, often difficult to know how much of this may be due to symbolism and how much to silver's intrinsic value.

While modern-day rituals, and the role of silver within them, are easier for us to understand, rituals and practices from the distant past are less clear to us and their symbolism can often only be guessed. For example, the Backworth Treasure, a hoard of Roman objects found in Britain in 1811, was deposited after AD 139 and included a chain, a bracelet, a number of rings, a pan, two brooches and three spoons. The

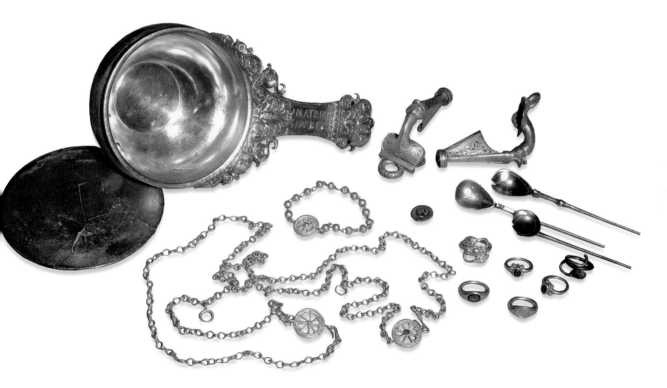

inscription on the pan – 'matr.fab dvbit' – suggests that the items were an offering to pagan mother goddesses, although the specific purpose of such votive offerings cannot now be established.

These items are similar to the large number of objects found in and around many sacred sites, where they may have been used in formal public rituals or placed there as a private offering. While most votive objects focus on the nature of the divine being in whose name they are offered, one group refers specifically to the situation of those making the offering. In some popular traditions, two- or three-dimensional images of body parts, made of silver, are placed at sacred sites in an effort to secure healing. Silver arms, legs, eyes and sometimes whole bodies have been found, apparently left in an attempt to alleviate blindness, lameness or other disabling or life-threatening ailments.

Silver anatomical votive made in Sicily around AD 1900–1940. L. 33 cm.

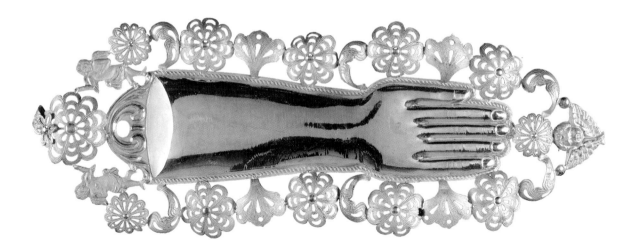

Amulets, unlike votive objects, are carried on the person, sometimes incorporated into an item of jewellery such as a bracelet or pendant. They are often made of precious metal or semi-precious stone and have symbolic meanings connected with human needs and the nature of the divine or magical powers with which they are associated. The aim is to provide some sort of protection, avert harm or to maintain good health or well-being. In ancient Egypt the scarab appears regularly, whether as a three-dimensional model (often in lapis) or in two-dimensional depictions. Associated with the dawning sun and rebirth, scarabs were placed over the hearts of the dead to protect them.

Scarab pendant from Egypt, around 1890 BC. H. 1.8 cm.

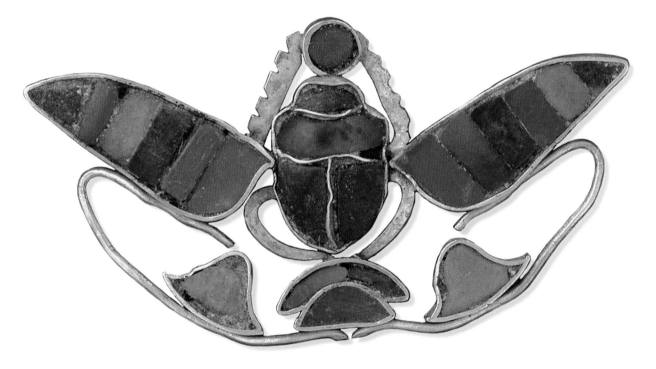

(right) Egyptian gold bracelet
with gold and silver amulets
dating from the Middle Kingdom
(1991–1785 BC). The figures
include a turtle, hare, snake,
baboon and falcon. Diam. 8 cm.

(below) Statuette of
Harpocrates dating from Roman
Britain, 1st to 2nd century AD.
Found by the Thames at London
Bridge. H. 6.5 cm.

An ancient Egyptian bracelet from the Middle Kingdom period
(1991–1785 BC) is made of two bands of gold, between which are
alternating silver and gold amulets. The animals and symbols were
probably intended to provide the wearer with the protection of the
deity they represent. Likewise it seems that a cast silver statuette of
Harpocrates (the Roman name for the Egyptian god Horus, son of the
powerful gods Isis and Osiris), dating from the first or second century
AD and found in the River Thames close to London Bridge, may have
been worn as an amulet, even if it seems rather large for this purpose,
since it has a gold chain and ring attached.

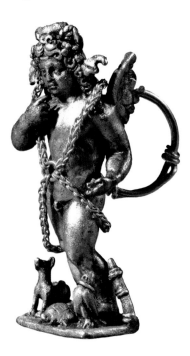

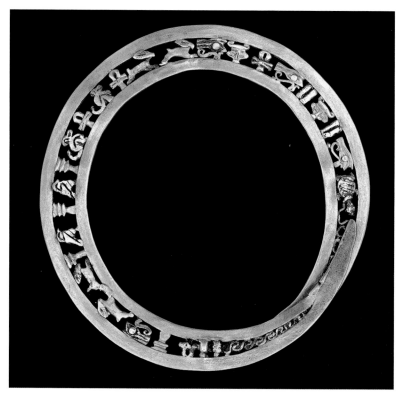

In early Middle Eastern and European cultures the wearing of jewellery in itself was considered protective and curative, though it seems that these properties were thought to be enhanced if the jewellery was made from precious metals. In later periods more specific pieces of silver were used to provide protection. A find from Nihavand in western Iran included an eleventh- or twelfth-century silver amulet case decorated with niello work and inscribed with a verse from the Qur'an. Silver crosses, crucifixes, St Christophers and Hands of Fatima, to name but a few examples, also date from this time, and people today continue to wear such items as expressions of their faith and a sense of divine protection.

Early silver Hand of Fatima from Biskra, Algeria.

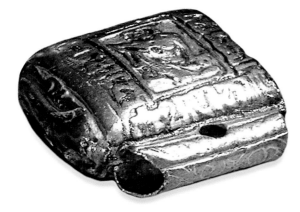

(left) Nielloed silver amulet case dating to the 11th–12th century AD, found with a cache of other objects in Nihavand, in western Iran. Both sides of the case are decorated in repoussé technique with a peacock, surrounded by an inscription of sura 112 of the Qur'an. The end of the case is decorated with a lion in high relief. L. 2.54 cm.

Chinese wedding charm in the form of a silver coin and ingot, 19th century AD.

The idea that the ownership of any small piece of silver may bring good luck has a long history. The silver charm bracelet has enjoyed popularity for many centuries. Silver is a traditional gift for a newborn baby – 'touching its hand' or 'crossing its palm' with silver is considered to have a magical power far in excess of the object's monetary value. Similarly, brides are traditionally presented with silver, not only as dowry but for luck and prosperity. This tradition crosses continents and centuries. A nineteenth-century Chinese silver wedding charm, incorporating a coin and an ingot, expresses the wish for both wealth and health, while British brides are sometimes offered an old silver sixpence coin to wear in their shoe for the same reason. This association between silver coinage and luck is a long one. In Britain, the withdrawal of the silver 'threepenny-bit' coin from circulation was a cause of some sadness to the many cooks who traditionally placed one in the middle of their Christmas pudding, for the extra good luck it conferred on whoever received that portion. Many people still turn over silver coins in their pocket while looking at a new moon, which is supposed to bring good luck.

Interestingly there is some evidence that silver indeed has protective properties – it is a natural antibiotic. Many sticking plasters and bandages now include silver, which they claim gives them greater healing power, as do some sports socks and shoes, as it kills the bacteria that leads to smelly feet. Water filters use silver as a purifying agent, perhaps prefigured by the Solomon's decree that the water containers in the Temple should be made of silver, and settlers of the American west used to drop a silver dollar into their water to keep it fresh overnight.

Silver is also often used to make or embellish objects for use in the more formal rituals of many religions, although the Islamic tradition uses glass, enamel, and pierced bronze rather than silver and gold. Some rituals use vessels to offer food and drink to the gods, either as propitiation or in response to their needs. Silver dishes and bowls, possibly for offering such libations, are typical not only in the ancient graves of Ur, but in Greek and Roman temples too.

In Tibetan Buddhist temples silver lamps fuelled with butter play a part in the offering rituals. Silver is also frequently used for the altar or sanctuary lamp which hangs above the tabernacle in Byzantine, Roman Catholic and High Anglican Christian traditions, but is more frequently used to make candle holders. For example, the nine-candle menorah, used during the Jewish festival of Hanukah, is commonly made from silver.

The scrolls of the Torah, used for public readings, are generally accompanied by a yad, a pointer with which to follow the words – to avoid any physical or symbolic harm caused by touching the scroll directly. The yad is usually made from silver, although it is not clear whether silver is employed for symbolic reasons or for its

(above) Silver libation bowl decorated with five chariots in relief, each driven by a winged Nike/Victory. In four of the chariots are deities, recognizable by what they wear or hold. Greek, around 300 BC, made in southern Italy; found at Èze, Alpes-Maritimes, southern France. Diam. 20.6 cm.

(left) Tibetan butter lamp with lotus petal design, used in the making of offerings. 18th or 19th century. H. 11.9 cm.

value or aesthetic qualities. Jewish ritual also includes the use of the Kiddush cup, the etrog box for spice, and the hand-washing cup, which are frequently made of, or decorated with, silver.

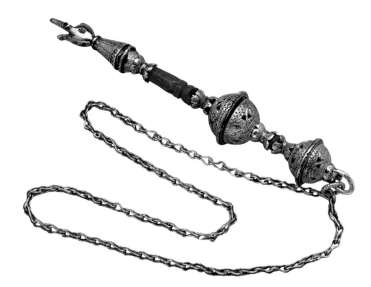

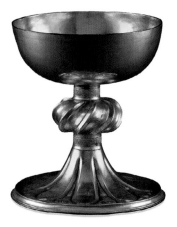

The Christian ritual of the Eucharist involves the symbolic use of bread and wine. Vessels used for the ritual include a chalice (wine) and paten (bread), a wine strainer and a pyx, for storing the consecrated bread, and are usually made from silver. A fourth-century Roman hoard unearthed at Water Newton in Huntingdonshire in 1975 contained nine vessels, several plaques and a gold disc, items that seem to carry symbolic force derived from quite different traditions. Some of the items have inscriptions or symbols clearly indicating that the pieces had a Christian use, although it is not certain whether the dishes and bowls were specifically connected with the Eucharist. The plaques, however, bear a close resemblance to those found in pagan temples bearing dedications to deities whose characteristics were honoured or invoked.

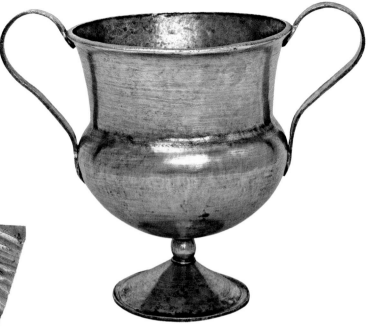

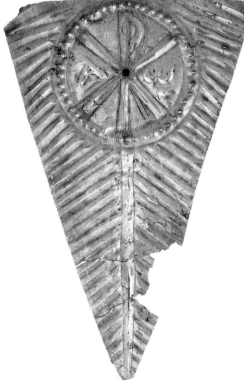

(above) Cup from the Water
Newton treasure. Roman
Britain, 4th century AD.
H. 12.5 cm.

(left) Silver plaque from the
Water Newton treasure, a blend
of traditions.
H. 15.7 cm.

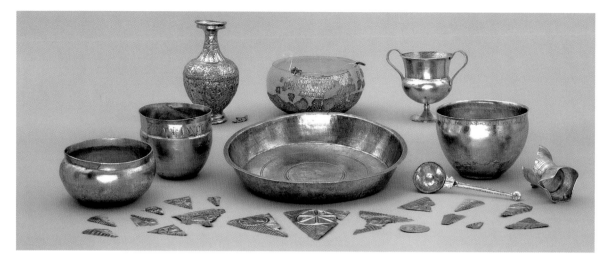

Throughout medieval Europe the Church was a major patron of metalworkers and many medieval smiths were also monks – St Dunstan, the patron saint of goldsmiths who famously tweaked the nose of the devil with his metalworking tongs, was a monk. By the early modern period, silver had become so closely connected with the Church that change in religious practices had a noticeable effect on the silver trade. At the time of the English Reformation, the ornate chalices from which only the priests drank were replaced by 'decent' communion cups, from which the whole congregation drank. Creating these replacements meant a great demand for the work of silversmiths. The Archbishop of Canterbury, Matthew Parker, took a close interest in these changes and made enquiries to ensure such replacements were made, keeping many local smiths in work and giving rise, some say, to the phrase 'nosey parker'. The old church plate and regalia was confiscated and sold. A Norwich silversmith paid £79 for the church plate from St Andrews, including crosses, chrismatories (to hold consecrated oils), censors, pyxes and chalices. It is said that there were parlours hung with altar cloths, tables and beds covered with copes, and chalices used for beer.

Silver objects are still given as gifts, especially to mark transitional events such as birth, christening, marriage or retirement. These gifts undoubtedly have a practical element, such as the provision of personal wealth, but also contain notions of rites of passage. The silver Projecta Casket, made in Rome about AD 380, is decorated with incised relief scenes, including processions possibly representing the bride's preparations, known to have traditionally taken place the evening before a Roman wedding. These scenes, and the fact that the casket is engraved with a Christian inscription: 'Secundus and Projecta, may you live in Christ', suggest that the casket was a wedding present.

The silver-gilt Projecta Casket, made in Rome around AD 380, possibly as a wedding present. L. 54.9 cm.

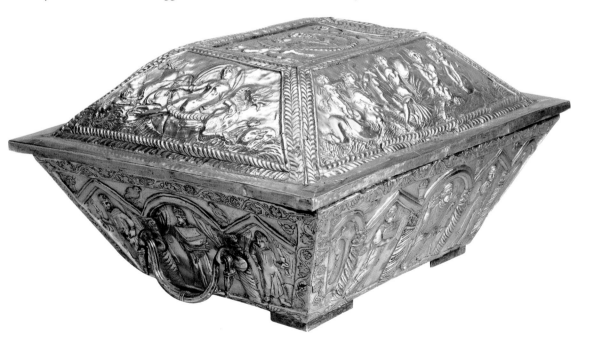

Contemporary photograph of
the King Edward VII Coronation
Cup, presented to the Brook Club.

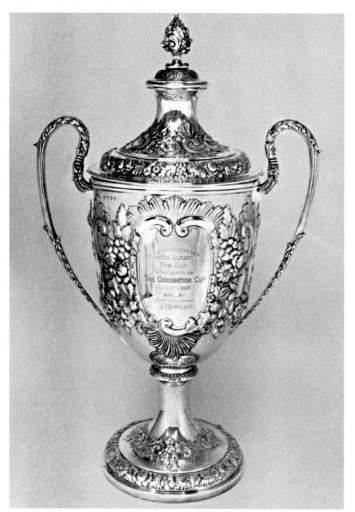

In the public as in the private realm, transitional events such as coronations and jubilees are occasions that are marked with the creation and donation of silver objects. For example in 1879 the Worshipful Company of Mercers ordered a number of plain silver salvers for distribution to its members on the occasion of Queen Victoria's Diamond Jubilee. In 1902 the Brook Club in New York was presented by a member, Mr Armour, with the King Edward VII Coronation Cup. This two-handled covered cup was originally won by Mr Armour in a yacht race across the English Channel from Cowes to Cherbourg and back. The Athenaeum Club in London displays a statue of Athena to commemorate Queen Elizabeth II's Golden Jubilee in 2003.

Livery companies and clubs have also traditionally been given gifts of silver from members perhaps, as with the King Edward Coronation Cup, to commemorate an event, or in acknowledgement of a particular favour. The Dutch Reformed Church of London presented a cup to the Mercers Company after they had been allowed to use the Mercers' Chapel for four years while their own church was being restored. These gifts can often encapsulate quite complex relationships. For example, in 1920 Mrs

May Cannan gave Trinity College, Oxford, a silver tea and coffee set in memory of her husband, who had been a tutor and also held college office. The service was originally a wedding present to the Cannans from his Trinity College undergraduates thirty years earlier.

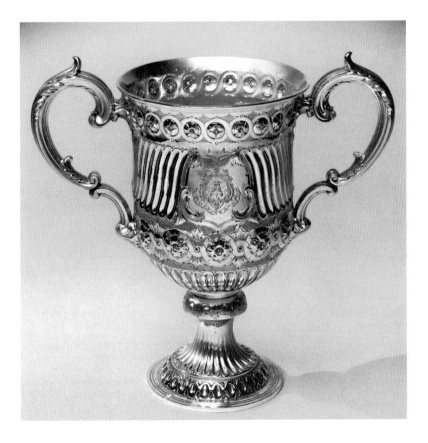

Contemporary photograph of the Dutch Cup, presented to the Mercers' Company by the Dutch Reformed Church of London.

6

Assaying and Hallmarking, Fakes and Forgeries

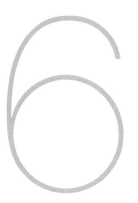

Silver ingot from 18th-century Burma with flowery patterns across its upper surface formed by exposure to a cooling current of air. The pattern only formed if the silver was of sufficient purity so the pattern was a mark of pure silver. Diam. 5.7 cm.

Given the importance of precious metals for the storage and transfer of wealth, and the reputation of smiths for their skill in the manipulation of metal and occasionally a little skulduggery, quality assurance has always been a matter of some importance. Deep scratches, punches or cuts are occasionally seen in older pieces of silver and were made in an attempt to establish the purity of the metal. This practice has been detected in pieces from ancient China, the Roman empire and the Anglo-Saxon world. In seventeenth- and eighteenth-century Burma, on the other hand, the purity of silver was guaranteed by a flowery pattern on the surface. This pattern was achieved by blowing cold air through a pipe on to the silver ingot as it cooled. Silver adulterated by too much copper would not form the right pattern.

Problems with the quality of silver arise from the fact that, unlike gold, silver rarely emerges from the earth in an almost pure state. Pure or 'fine' silver must first be separated from other substances and

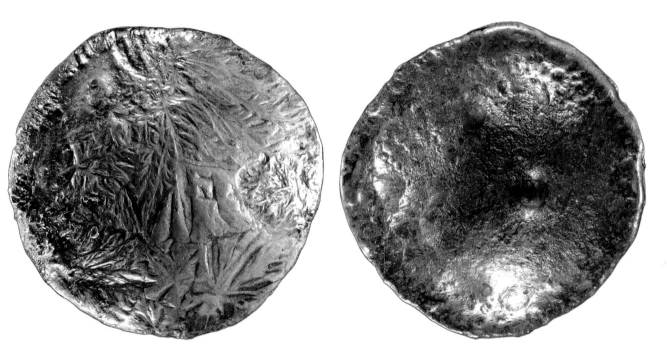

refined. Secondly, even when fine silver has been produced, it is quite soft and must be mixed in the right proportions, traditionally with copper, to achieve the required tensile strength for most purposes. It has therefore long been acknowledged that a standard for the alloy was needed.

Silver standards

One system of silver quality guarantee, which has been in continuous operation for seven hundred years, is that of the London – and other British – Assay Offices. Its hallmarking system began to be developed in AD 1300 and was complete, in principle, by the following century. Details of methods, administration and sanctions have changed, but the principles remain the same.

One theory for the origin of the sterling standard is that when in the twelfth century the English coinage was reformed by Henry II he employed German metal refiners, known as 'Esterlings'. The standard they employed for the new coinage, which would later be extended from coins to all silver goods, was named after them, as sterling. In 1238 it was decreed that the coinage should be tested periodically against this standard by six 'faithful and discreet' goldsmiths from London ('discreet' implying independent). This process of testing the coinage became known as the Trial of the Pyx.

Since silver goods as well as coinage were used in trade, in 1300 Edward I decided to address the purity of silverware. He decreed that no silver item should be sold unless it had been tested ('assayed') by chosen members of what was later to become the Worshipful Company of Goldsmiths. Each piece assayed in this way was to be marked with a leopard's head. This process was the beginning of the self-regulation of the gold and silver trade, designed to offer protection – both to the public and to honest workers – from the practices of less scrupulous smiths. Since that time the Assay Offices have to a large extent drawn their personnel from and been administered by the Worshipful Company of Goldsmiths.

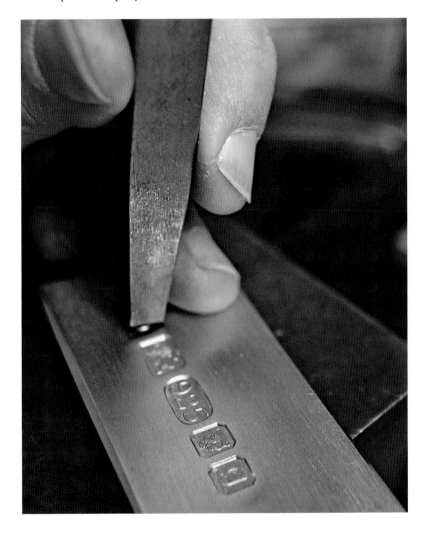

Hallmarking.

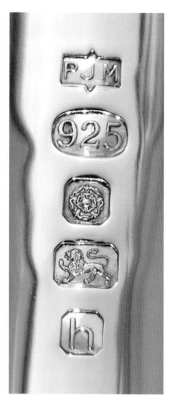

Hallmark showing (top to bottom) the sponsor's mark, the standard of silver, two marks showing the assay office that tested the item and the date letter indicating the year the piece was assayed, and therefore the assay master resonsible.

By 1363 it had been decided that items should not only bear the assay mark but that of the maker, usually his initials. By the mid fifteenth century a letter mark was added in order to establish who had been the warden responsible for the marking at a particular time, since a statute of 1423 ensured that wardens were to be penalized if they were found to have marked substandard goods. The new mark, a letter within a shield known as the assayer's mark, was changed each year upon the appointment of a new warden. Ever since, letters from A to Z of varying styles in different shields have been used to signify the date of marking. As companies of goldsmiths and silversmiths in cities other than London acquired the right to establish halls to assay local work, these too acquired their own marks, so that each piece of silver now carries four obligatory marks – the assay mark, ensuring the quality; the maker's or sponsor's mark, signifying who is responsible for the manufacture; and the hall and date marks, indicating where and when the piece was tested.

This seems straightforward, but there were centuries of dispute as to how these regulations and their sanctions would be applied. It took some time to establish whether they applied outside London – in the fifteenth century, Norwich and Ipswich thought not. Regulations were introduced requiring 'foreign' workers (from the provinces and abroad) to work in the open streets and to be subject to wardens' checks of their workshops. Regulations were unclear as to the status of migrant workers and imported goods. In addition, there was a problem concerning goods too small to mark. This applied particularly to silver and gold thread (important in court circles) and to chains and small work which had no flat surfaces on which to display marks. Notwithstanding these difficulties, small-workers were brought within the act in 1696 and hallmarking was made compulsory throughout the country in 1697. In the early years the wardens, and later the assay master, took a rather proactive approach to their responsibilities, searching shops and fairs and visiting workshops, as well as receiving pieces brought to them. By whatever means work arrived at the assay office, it was their task to establish its silver content. Two methods were used, the first involving a touchstone and the second relying on extreme temperatures.

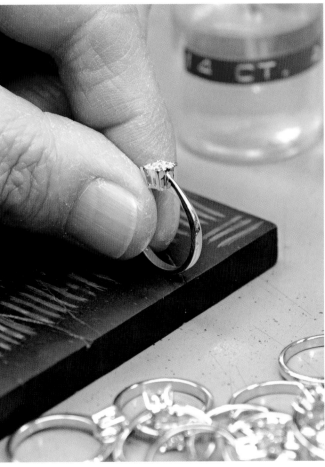

Touchstone assaying.

Testing silver by use of a touchstone dates from well before the existence of the London Assay Office. The article to be tested was rubbed on a black stone (originally basanite), leaving a streak of metal behind. The streak was then compared with samples of a pre-established standard, displayed on a series of touch needles rather like a colour chart. In more recent times chemicals were applied to the streak, and from the reaction that took place a first impression of the fineness of the metal could be gained. One such stone was excavated from a seventh-century Anglo-Saxon cemetery in Kent.

The method of 'touching', while quick and easy, was not altogether accurate or quantifiable. Cupellation dates back to pre-Roman times and offered more precise results. Samples of gold and silver were accurately weighed and then wrapped in lead foil and rolled into a ball. This was put into a cupel (a small cup made of bone ash), which was then placed into a furnace and heated to 1100°C until all the metals except the gold and silver had been absorbed into the material of the cupel. A sphere of gold and silver remained, and the silver was separated out by the use of nitric acid. This allowed the degree of purity of both the silver and the gold samples to be calculated with 99.9 per cent accuracy (providing that accurate weights were available at the outset). In more recent years

Cupellation tray.

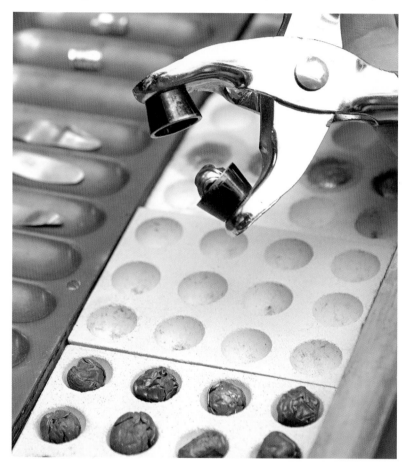

highly sophisticated chemical and electronic methods have been developed. 'Titration', for example, achieves chemically the same degree of accuracy as cupellation, but without the use of a furnace. Once passed, by whatever method, the items were (and still are) stamped with steel punches made especially for the Assay Office by skilled engravers and die makers.

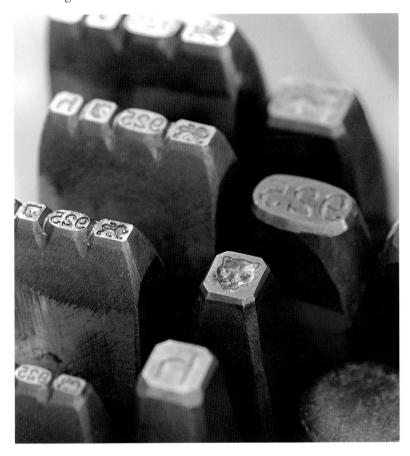

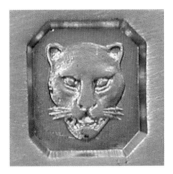

Hallmarking punches with the leopard's head mark of the London Assay Office (below).

In the event of the sample failing, early wardens and assay masters had various sanctions at their disposal. The first and most immediate of these was to break the piece so that it could not be sold. After that they could impose fines, merely for having made a substandard item, even if at that point it had not been offered for sale. One ordinance of the Worshipful Company of Goldsmiths set down that first offences attracted a fine of two shillings, second offences six shillings and third offences twenty shillings. Alternative punishments could include prison, public naming and shaming in the stocks in front of the Goldsmiths' Hall, or being refused the right to have goods assayed, which effectively put the culprit out of business or banished him beyond the reach of the Goldsmiths' Company.

Making substandard materials or goods, or offering them for sale, were not the only practices specifically prohibited by law. Far more serious was the counterfeiting of hallmarks and the adding to or alteration of pieces, giving them uses other than their original ones. Offences of this nature attracted much greater penalties, including hard labour, transportation and occasionally death.

Despite these punishments, smiths were tempted to flout the rules for several reasons such as cutting corners to increase profit, the time and expense involved in sending the pieces for assay, or the introduction of 'plate duty' on the sale of silver in 1720. It became a great temptation either not to have pieces marked or to have the lightest possible piece marked. Another reason for alteration of silver items was the result of the increasing interest in antiquities and collecting. By the sixteenth century in Europe new attitudes to silver were beginning to emerge, replacing the old belief in the intrinsic value of the metal (if it was pure and heavy, it was good). The changing attitudes, increasingly pronounced in the seventeenth, eighteenth and nineteenth centuries through to the present day, had two strands. The first was a growing interest in items associated with royal or noble households or more generally considered 'of importance'. The second was a fascination with antiquity. As wealthy families, the Church, colleges and institutions sold off their old plate in favour of less worn and more fashionable items, they entered new collections.

By the eighteenth century the sideboard, with its display not only of silver but also porcelain and glass, had taken over from the buffet, and old pieces reminiscent of that former magnificence were given pride of place. By the nineteenth century the Victoria and Albert Museum was collecting examples of old British silver, and the 1862 South Kensington Exhibition featured pieces of silver borrowed for the occasion. Old silver had acquired a value divorced from its weight amongst a newly wealthy middle class. The demand for pieces of this sort greatly exceeded the supply, creating the conditions for illegal attempts to fill the gap.

Fakes and forgeries

These four factors – businesses cutting corners; workers avoiding inconvenience; 'duty dodging'; and responding to the growing and lucrative demands of collectors and the antiques market – accounted for the emergence of fakes and forgeries. The least sophisticated fakes and the easiest to spot include the use of plated base metals instead of solid silver and the production of bogus hallmarks, often by the repetition of the maker's mark, which it was hoped would fool the ill-informed and those with weak eyesight. Sometimes too there was excessive use of solder in the manufacture of joints, which lowered the overall silver content of the piece.

Some of the practices that followed the introduction of plate duty were rather more sophisticated. During these periods the weight of silver sent to the Assay Office determined the duty to be paid by the smith – so it made financial sense to send as little as possible. It did not take great ingenuity to send in a relatively light beaker and add the

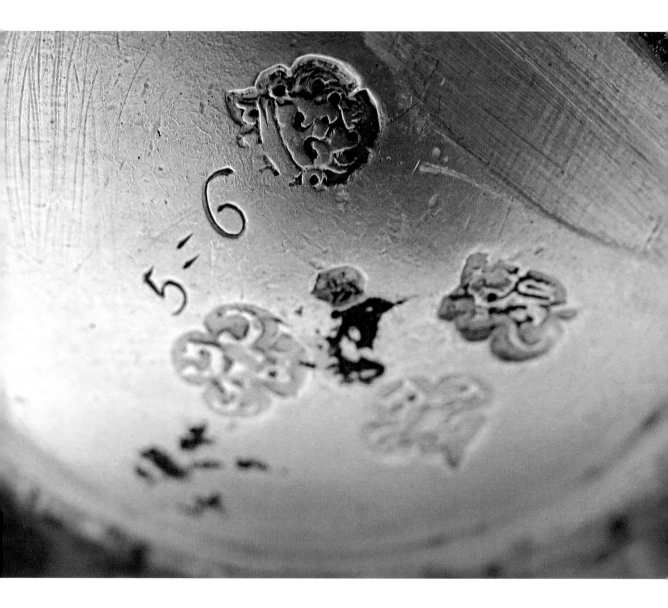

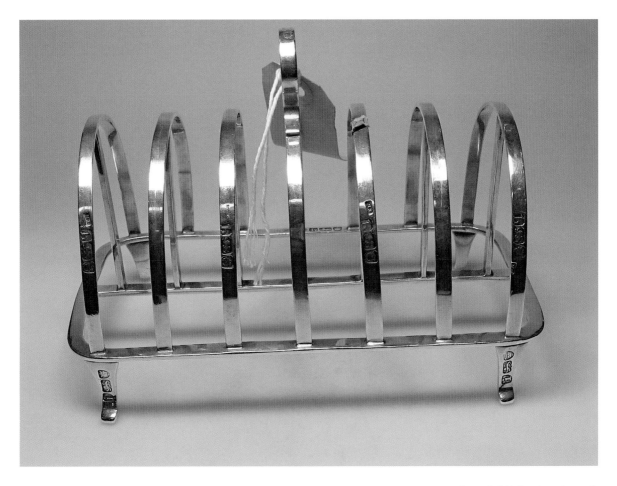

(opposite) Hallmark made up of repeated maker's marks.

(above) Toast-rack made from stretched, hallmarked silver spoon handles.

handle, spout and lid when it was returned, turning it into a coffee pot. Other evasive tactics, either to dodge tax or to prevent the discovery of substandard goods, usually involved not sending the silver to the Assay Office at all and either transposing or forging a hallmark.

Transposing an existing genuine hallmark requires cutting it from a smaller or broken object and soldering it into the new, larger one. Forging hallmarks can be done in several ways. An existing object which has already been hallmarked could be copied and cast in its entirety, hallmark and all. Alternatively, counterfeit punches could be produced and the piece stamped illegally. However, apart from the risk of being found in possession of such a punch, producing a convincing one would be extremely difficult as the skill involved is quite specialized.

Transposed hallmarks.

Unless contemplating fraud on a massive scale, it would be cheaper not to try. Finally, there is a method known as 'soft punching'. A rod of a softer metal such as copper is heated at the end until it is on the verge of melting. At this point it is pressed into a genuine hallmark and allowed to cool with the impression of the mark on it. A punch of this sort would replicate the mark reasonably convincingly, at least to the inexperienced eye, but it could only be used two or three times before it lost the necessary sharpness.

The prices paid for pieces associated with the glory, magnificence, nobility or curiosity of the past have led to the counterfeiting of objects to fulfil the desires of collectors and antiquarians. This characteristically involved the engraving of bogus coats of arms and inscriptions, and sometimes the addition of ornamentation to imply a different, more sought-after, age or style.

In 1939, to combat the problem of fakes, the London Assay Office drew together a small group of experts, all highly qualified and experienced professional scientists, academics, smiths and collectors, and created the Antique Plate Committee. Its duty is to decide on the authenticity of antique silver brought before it, if that silver is thought to be in some way suspect. The Committee can draw upon experience and knowledge as well as scientific analytical techniques. It can look for anachronisms – such as modern 'clean' metal with few extraneous impurities in 'old' pieces, and solder containing specific, controlled quantities of cadmium, a development designed to make it flow more effectively into joints but which was subsequently outlawed for health reasons.

If the standard of workmanship is high, forgeries may go undetected at the time they are perpetrated. While fakes and forgeries come to light from time to time, tracing them back to the source is not always easy. This is especially true when a piece comes on to the market years, if not centuries, after it was produced. For example, there is a footed platter with the authentic marks of Paul Storr and the London Assay Office stamped on the underside. This would be a rare piece that could be expected to command a high price in any antique silver auction. The problem is that Paul Storr only made half of it. He made a number of quite plain plates, one of which had presumably become separated from a set. By itself it would not be particularly valuable, but with the addition of three elaborate feet and ornate swags festooning the rim it would be deemed rare and expensive. Whenever there is the likelihood of very large amounts of money changing hands, there is also the danger of deception of one sort or another. Silver, undoubtedly a store of wealth, may also be a lure to the acquisitive.

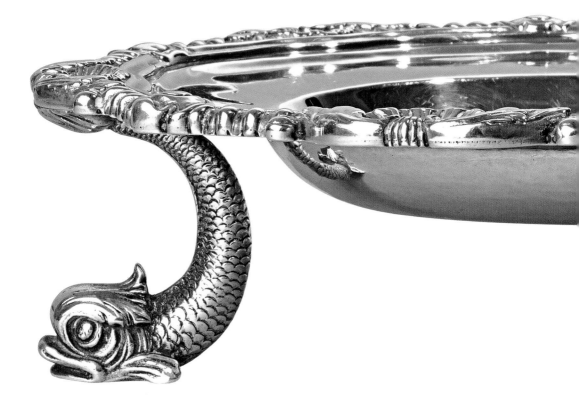

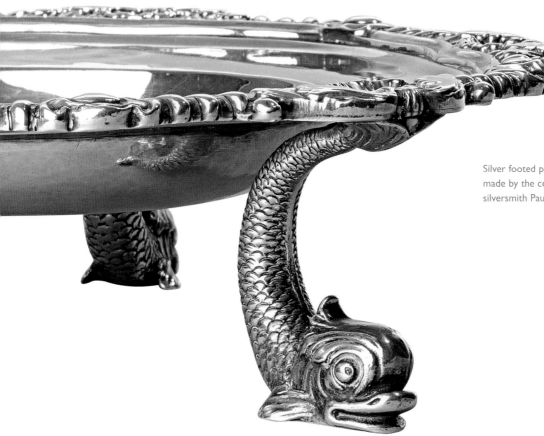

Silver footed platter supposedly made by the celebrated silversmith Paul Storr.

7

Tools and Techniques

The crafting of most silver pieces relies on a combination of techniques that fall into four main categories: cutting, forming, joining and polishing. To these may be added various decorative techniques. The sequence in which these processes are involved varies, although polishing always comes last.

Cutting techniques

Cutting includes any process that changes the amount of metal present, by removing part of it mechanically.

Drilling

The earliest known silver artefacts are beads, and the difference between a bead and a blob of silver is the hole in the middle. Early drilling was achieved by rotating a hard, sharp object on the same spot at speed, and once it was possible to make a hole it was possible to string things together for decoration. There are pictures on the walls of Egyptian tombs of bow drills of identical design to those found in medieval engravings, in descriptions of eighteenth-century workbenches and on sale in current silversmithing tool catalogues.

Engraving

Early smiths had the tools with which to cut, or undercut, the surface of metal either for decorative or structural reasons. Decorating the surface of metal by gouging out channels with hard, facetted, tools was practised in Mesopotamia as early as the second millennium BC. Cutting channels into which other metals could be inlaid was a technique known and frequently practised at least as early as fourth-century Iran.

Grinding and filing

Abrasive stones have always been used to remove the surface layer of a worked piece of silver in order to smooth it or to remove the surface oxidization (fire stain). While modern smiths may use abrasive wheels driven by electric motors, earlier smiths would rub the stones directly on to the surface of the work, or grind the abrasive material into a fine dust and mix it with tallow to form a block of the desired shape. The other common way of changing the shape of a piece of metal, usually to get rid of lumps too small or inconveniently positioned to use a saw, is to file it. The Romans used files, and while the modern versions may offer a wider choice of gauges and cuts, the principle remains the same.

Sawing

Saws are used to cut through sheet silver. The principle of the saw blade has not changed in 5000 years, though the precision with which it can be made clearly has. When blades were cast in copper in 3050 BC they needed to be fairly large, with teeth at least as large as the grains of the medium in which they were cast. Furthermore, because they were cast they would have been brittle. The modern silversmith uses tempered steel blades, which are hardened and springy, with a choice of gauge usually beginning at four teeth to the millimetre.

Forming techniques

Forming involves shaping a given quantity of metal, or changing the shape of a piece of metal, without altering its weight.

Casting

This is the technique of pouring molten metal into prepared moulds, and has been in use for at least 6000 years. Modern moulds for silver tend to be made of quick-setting plaster or silicone compounds, but earlier methods made use of limestone, bone, sand and clay. The earliest method, 'open moulding', involved carving a shape in a stone or impressing a shape into a softer material, such as sand or clay, and then pouring in the molten metal so that the resulting object had one flat side and one bearing the features of the object carved or impressed. A later development was the creation of a mould in two halves that could cast fully modelled objects.

Lost wax casting

The 'lost wax' casting method was developed in antiquity but is still the predominant method used today. A wax model is made and coated with clay or plaster with a channel left for the molten silver to enter and small vents for the expelled air to escape. The wax is then melted out, and molten silver poured into the cavity left by the wax.

Core casting

A refinement of this is 'core casting', a method of casting holloware (containers or receptacles), probably first used by the Chinese in casting vast bronze water vessels. Here a shape corresponding to the empty inside of the vessel is formed of clay. This is covered with a layer of wax slightly thicker than the desired thickness of the vessel. A second layer of clay surrounds the wax. The two volumes of clay, the inner and the outer walls of the vessel, are located in relation to each other by pins passing through the wax. The clay is dried, the wax burned out, the silver introduced into the space left by the wax and the baked clay removed, leaving a hollow vessel shape (punctured by holes where the locating pins were, which are then filled in).

Hammering and raising

The most straightforward way of forming or shaping a piece of silver is to hit it with something hard. In fact the word 'malleable' comes from the Latin word for a hammer. Refined silver would begin life either as an irregular blob or as an ingot, so the first task would be to use a hammer to flatten the silver into a sheet. Thereafter, depending on the item to be produced, the sheet could be hammered on a flat surface to make it flatter or on a curved surface with a domed hammer face to curve it. For instance, the process of raising a bowl involves repeatedly hammering a disc of silver over a former (a stake), with a circular series of hammer strokes working round and round from the centre to the edge until the flat disc becomes a dish and then a bowl. Egyptian grave vessels were formed in this way, creating hollow vessels without the need for making any seams. It was many centuries before other methods of construction evolved.

Forging

Traditionally, the other way of forming a three-dimensional silver object was to forge it. Solid and complex shapes can be produced by hammering an ingot. Weapons and tools were early products of this method – indeed Vulcan is portrayed at his forge making weaponry for the gods – and we hear of swords being beaten into plough shares. All that is required for forging silver is a hammer and an anvil, since the silver is worked cold and therefore does not need to be held with tongs. The earliest hammers were probably made of stones with both a flat and a curved surface, which could be applied to silver placed on a flat stone used as an anvil. The principle of forging is one of stretching and compression. If a piece, such as a spoon bowl, is to have a wide surface it is hammered repeatedly on that surface. If there is to be a thickened neck to the handle, it is hammered on the edge to compress the metal in that section. Sharp edges are achieved by repeated blows near to the edge. In recent centuries forging has been the preferred method of producing the best-quality cutlery, proving ideal for this purpose since hammering not only allows for fine discriminations of thickness, but hardens the work, increasing its strength and springiness.

Spinning

Hollow vessels can be produced by mounting a disc of silver on a lathe and forcing it over a form while it spins. This is a quick and efficient method of production, but one that requires a great deal of power: the disc needs to rotate about a thousand times a minute for this to work. Although some pieces, such as the seventh-century Sutton Hoo dishes, bear circular marks which suggest that they might have been spun, this seems unlikely given the lathe technology involved. Only later is there firm evidence of the spinning of numerous, absolutely symmetrical, objects.

Stamping

Stamping, that is imprinting a design by forcing a die on to a piece of cold silver, or forcing the silver into a die, was known at least as early as the first coinage, and was a technique certainly in use by the seventh century BC. The only limitation was the amount of force it was possible to exert with accuracy. For this reason large-scale stamping and pressing only came into its own with the industrial harnessing of power derived from coal and water, and with the manufacturing of heavy machinery and steel dies capable of stamping out larger objects at one blow. Eighteenth- and nineteenth-century silver production was characterized by the use of the stamping press, turning out a profusion of domestic items and personal accessories.

Joining techniques

In many cases it is not possible to make a silver object from a single piece of metal. Although pieces of metal can be fused together by melting the two and pressing them together, rivetting and soldering are the two main methods of joining metals. Once it is possible to join two pieces of metal successfully, all sorts of design options become a possibility.

Rivetting

Rivetting has been available for as long as it has been possible to drill holes. The two elements to be joined are overlapped, a hole is drilled through both of them, and a rod of the same diameter inserted. The protruding ends of the rod are then hammered flat on each side, squeezing the two surfaces together and spreading the ends of the rod slightly to prevent it from slipping out. The huge advantage of riveting is that it doesn't require heat, so it is ideal in circumstances where the elements are either too large to heat to the right temperature or where one of the elements to be joined is flammable (for instance, wood, horn, bone or leather). This method is therefore used for securing wooden handles to vessels, decorations to leather belts and harnesses, and silver bindings to horn vessels. However this method has one particular disadvantage – it is not easy to make watertight joints.

Soldering

Soldering involves fitting pieces of silver together as closely as possible and then placing small pieces of the solder over the joints. A silver solder is a metal alloy with a lower melting point than that of the pieces of silver that are to be joined. When the pieces are heated the solder alloy melts quickly and forming a bond by fusing with each silver surface. Ancient smiths used a copper alloy, sometimes with tin or lead, to solder silver. The soldering process was made easier by the nineteenth-century discovery that introducing a flux of ground borax into the joint encouraged the flow of the solder. Once soldering had been mastered, bowls could have stems and bases, pots could have handles and spouts, square boxes could be constructed, and heavy, cast decorations could be applied to otherwise plain surfaces.

Decorative techniques

Space precludes more than a brief mention of the numerous decorative techniques that have been available to the silversmith for around five millennia. Silver has been set with stones, gilded, enamelled and inlaid with other metals. Here there is room only to describe briefly two of the most frequently used techniques.

Niello

Niello work is the production of a black design on a silver surface that creates richly decorative results without the significant use of materials other than silver compounds. The earliest method involved engraving a design into the surface of the silver and embedding a form of silver sulphide, blackened by the lead and sulphur in the mixture, into the recesses. Silver sulphide becomes malleable at a temperature far below its melting point and can be inlaid into the engraved channels before being heated gently and burnished flush with the surface of the rest of the work. This method, well known to the

Romans, was adapted initially by Arab workers in the Middle Ages when the recipe was altered to consist of four parts of silver, two of copper, one of lead and some sulphur. This proved more acceptable, since it provided the visual contrast required.

Repoussé and Chasing

Both repoussé and chasing involve moving the surface of an object with a variety of fine hammers and punches. Chasing involves working on the front, while repoussé work involves pushing the metal up from the back. There are some remarkable examples where only one method has been used, for example the Corbridge Lanx, an ornate decorative tray from Roman Britain, where the surface metal has been moved around with a series of hand punches to produce the most marvellous and complex representational designs. Here the effect is achieved by rendering the design in high relief – the reverse is flat and has not been worked. Normally, though, a combination of work from the front and from the back is involved. Surfaces that have been raised from behind will be highlighted, often outlined, from the front, providing added definition to the contours created by the repoussé work.

Recent technical advances

Plating had been used in one form or another since the sixth century BC. The Romans had soldered thin sheets of silver foil to base metals and had applied molten silver alloys to the surface of other metals. By the first century AD the Chinese had discovered the possibility of applying a mercury-silver amalgam to surfaces. However, the harnessing of electricity accounted for the rapid growth of techniques such as electroplating, electro-stripping and electroforming. Michael Faraday discovered the principles of electroplating in the mid-nineteenth century. This process consists of allowing an electric current to flow between two metals acting as electrodes through a solution. The current flow causes charged metal particles to pass from one electrode to the other.

This has three main applications for silversmiths. The first is to deposit a layer of silver on to the surface of another metal. The second is to strip the surface layer containing impurities such as oxidized copper, from a silver object. The third application is electroforming, whereby silver objects are formed from metal or non-metal models by the repeated deposition of layers of silver on the surface of the model. While creating a grainy, rather organic-looking quality in the pieces, which has made it highly fashionable in the production of naturally inspired craft works, this is an extremely time-consuming method of generating three-dimensional objects.

Polishing

Perhaps predictably, the processes of polishing have not altered significantly during the history of silversmithing. Although the electric motor has made the work easier, the principles and processes remain the same. Electro-stripping can remove fire stain, but cleaning is different from polishing. Polishing is the process of removing scratches by the application of finer and finer abrasives. Coarse abrasives, such as emery, remove the deeper scratches but leave smaller ones. These in turn are removed by pumice or ash, and the finer scratches left by these are then removed by an even finer compound. The finest polishing agent is normally rouge, a compound of red iron oxide and grease. After its use no visible scratches remain and the piece acquires a mirror finish. For many lovers of silver this can only improved by the softer patina achieved by many years of gentle handling and buffing.

Acknowledgements

Many people have been generous with their time during the preparation of Silver. The British Museum's curatorial, scientific and conservation staff offered numerous useful suggestions in the early stages of the project and saved me from committing errors of both fact and interpretation later on. More than one member of the editorial staff of British Museum Press has provided support and encouragement, keeping a clear eye on the final outcome of the various discussions and drafts. Janet Ford read the text as it was produced and must accept much of the credit for such clarity as exists.

Gary Haines and Mark Clark of the Mercers' Company provided access to the Mercers' Company silver vaults, together with a wealth of fascinating information. Emma Shipley provided the same service at the Royal College of Physicians, providing access to the silver collection and to their records. John Kirkup shared his encyclopedic knowledge of the development of surgical instruments in a most helpful way.

Ongoing discussions with fellow silversmiths have, of course, informed my understanding of the various technical processes referred to, as have the technical bulletins made available by the Worshipful Company of Goldsmiths.

It has been a delight to have been brought into contact with so many people who are so passionate about what they do.

Suggestions for Further Reading

The text of this book draws heavily on other people's wisdom and research. The following works deal in full with many of the ideas raised here.

General

Allan, J. M., *Islamic Metalwork*, London 1982

Althaus, F. and Sutcliffe, M. (eds), *The Road to Byzantium*, London 2006

Barsali, I. B., *Medieval Goldsmiths' Work*, London 1966

Bennett, D., *Collecting Irish Silver*, London 1984

Blair, C. (ed.), *The History of Silver*, London 1987

Cripps, W. J., *Old English Plate: Ecclesiastical, Decorative and Domestic*, London 1886

Curtis, J., *Ancient Persia*, London 2000

Evans, A. C., *The Sutton Hoo Ship Burial*, London 2002

Falino, J. and Ward, G. W. R., *New England Silver and Silversmithing 1620–1815*, Boston 2001

Glanville, P., *Silver in England*, London 1987

Hartop, C. (ed.), *East Anglian Silver 1550–1750*, Cambridge 2004

Hawley, R., *Omani Silver*, London 1984

Jansson, I. (ed.), *The Viking Heritage: A Dialogue between Cultures*, Stockholm 1996

Pickford, I., *Silver Flatware: English, Irish and Scottish, 1660–1980*, Woodbridge 1983

Truman, C., (ed.), *Sotheby's Concise Encyclopedia of Silver*, London 1993

Ward, R., *Islamic Metalwork*, London 1993

Youngs, S., *The Work of Angels*, London 1990

Value and Wealth

Clifford, H. M., *A Treasured Inheritance: 600 Years of Oxford College Silver*, Oxford 2004

Eagleton, C. and Williams, J. (eds), *Money: A History*, London 1997

Graham-Campbell, J. and Williams, G. (eds), *Silver Economy in the Viking Age*, Tucson 2005

Lane, R., *The Mercers' Company Plate*, London 1985

Reece, R., *Coinage of Roman Britain*, Stroud 2002

Silver and Status

Dmitrieva, O. and Abromova, N. (eds), *Britannia and Muscovy: English Silver at the Court of the Tsars*, New Haven and London 2006

Glanville, P., *Silver in Tudor and Early Stuart England*, London 1990

Marzinzik, S., *The Sutton Hoo Helmet*, London 2007

McFadden, D. R., *Treasures for the Table: Silver from the Chrysler Museum*, New York 1989

Tiradritti, F., *Egyptian Treasures from the Egyptian Museum in Cairo*, New York 1999

Adornment

Hughes, G., *The Art of Jewellery*, London 1972

Johns, C., *The Jewellery of Roman Britain: Celtic and Classical Traditions*, London 1996

Mason, S., *Jewellery Making in Birmingham 1750–1995*, Chichester 1998

Tait, H. (ed.), *7000 Years of Jewellery*, 3rd edn, London 2006

Ture, A. and Savascin, M. Y., *Antique Jewellery of Anatolia*, Istanbul 2002

Silversmiths

Braham, H., *A Century of Silver: The Courtauld Family of Silversmiths 1710–1780*, London 2003

Cellini, Benvenuto, trans. Symonds, J. A., *Autobiography*, New York 2001

Cherry, J., *Medieval Craftsmen: Goldsmiths*, London 1992

Culme, J., 'Paul Storr', *Oxford Dictionary of National Biography*, Oxford 2004

Dasen, V., *Dwarfs in Ancient Egypt and Greece*, Oxford 1993

Glanville, P. and Goldsborough, J. F., *Women Silversmiths 1685–1845*, London 1990

McLanathan, R. B. K. (ed.), *Colonial Silversmiths: Masters and Apprentices*, Boston 1956

Triber, J. E., *A True Republican: The Life of Paul Revere*, Amherst 1998

Symbolic Value

Boyd, S. A. and Mango, M. (eds), *Ecclesiastical Silver Plate in Sixth Century Byzantium*, Cambridge, MA 1992

Leader-Newby, R. E., *Silver and Society in Late Antiquity: Functions and Meanings of Silver Plate in the Fourth to Seventh Centuries*, London 2004

Rogers, S., *Power and Gold: Jewelry from Indonesia, Malaysia, and the Philippines*, 3rd edn, Geneva 1995

Suarez, D., Rodgers, O. and Holden, P., *The Collection of Silver and Pewter belonging to The Brook*, New York 1966

Williams, D., *The Warren Cup*, London 2006

Assaying, Hallmarking, Fakes and Forgeries

Forbes, J. S., *Hallmark: A History of the London Assay Office*, London 1998

The Goldsmiths' Company, *Spurious Antique Plate*, London 1899

Johnson, P. V. A., 'The Lyon and Twinam Forgeries', *The Proceedings of the Silver Society*, vol. III, nos 1–2, 1983

Kürkman, G., *Ottoman Silver Marks*, New York 1996

Tait, H., 'Old Silver and the Law', The Antique Collector, April 1989

Tann, J., *Birmingham Assay Office, 1773–1993*, Birmingham 1993

Tools, Techniques and Metal Technology

Allan, J. M., *Persian Metal Technology 700–1300*, London 1979

Craddock, P. and Lang, J. (eds), *Mining and Metal Production through the Ages*, London 2003

Curtis, L., *Electroforming*, London 2004

Maryon, H., *Metalwork and Enamelling*, London 1971

McCreight, T., *The Complete Metalsmith* (Professional Edition), Portland, ME 2005

Petrie, W. M. F., *Tools and Weapons*, London 1917

Scheel, B., *Egyptian Metalworking and Tools*, Aylesbury 1989

Untracht, O., *Metal Techniques for Craftsmen*, Garden City, New York 1968

Illustration Acknowledgements

Illustrations are © The Trustees of the British Museum except where otherwise noted.

page

2 P&E 1952,0404.1 (Given by Capt. A.W. Francis)
4 GR 1891,0627.3
7 P&E 1946,1007.1
8 ME 1973,0120.1
9 GR 1853,0314.1
10 CM 1906,1103.2591 (Given by Dr F. Parkes Weber)
11 P&E 1979,1102.1
12 P&E 1994,0408.30 (Purchased with the assistance of the National Heritage Memorial Fund, the Art Fund and the British Museum Friends)
15 ME 1967,0617.1
16 (top) AES 1974,0223.1 (below) CM 1878,0301.384
17 CM 1998,1101
18 CM 1893,1108.7 (Given by S.H. Augier)
19 P&E 1855,0815.1–31
20 CM 1839,0130.5 (Given by Mrs Richards)
21 ASIA As2002,04.10
22 ASIA As1968,04.5
23 CM 1983,0101
24 P&E 1859,0511.1–11
25 P&E 1841,0711/CM 1838,0710 (Given by H.M. Queen Victoria)
26 P&E 1991,0407.39

27 (top) With the kind permission of the Principal, Fellows and Scholars of Jesus College, Oxford (below) Queen's College, Oxford
28 (top) Magdalen College, Oxford (below) Queen's College, Oxford
29 The Mercers' Company
31 ME 1964,0713.1
32 ME 1929,1017.2
33 Egyptian Museum, Cairo
34 P&E 1939,1010.79–81 & 88–9 (Given by Mrs E.M. Pretty)
35 P&E 1965,0705.1–5
36 P&E 1992,0614.1–26 (Purchased with the assistance of the National Heritage Memorial Fund)
38 P&E 1969,0705.3 & 25 (Bequeathed by Peter Wilding)
39 London Assay Office
41 P&E 1981,1003.1–2
42 Photograph: Andy Barker, Communications, Sheffield City Council
45 P&E 1978,1002.312 (Given by Professor and Mrs Hull Grundy)
46 (left) ME 1929,1017.114–130.a (right) ASIA 1938,0524.284
47 (left) P&E 1907,0520.13 (Given by J. Pierpont Morgan) (right) The Museum of National Antiquities, Stockholm
48 P&E 1986,0401.320
49 P&E 1932,0706.2
50 The Museum of National Antiquities, Stockholm
51 Birmingham Museum and Art Gallery
52 P&E 1850,1106.1–4
53 P&E 1905,0520.222

54 (left) P&E 1888,0719.102 (right) P&E 1909,0624.2
55 (top) P&E 1859,0511.2 (bottom left) P&E 1883,0401.176 (Given by Sir A.W. Franks) (bottom right) P&E 1888,0719.100
56 P&E 1888,0719.101
57 P&E 1952,0404.1 (Given by Capt. A.W. Francis)
58 (top) P&E 1893,0601.204 (middle) P&E 1891,1019.1 (bottom) P&E AF.2811 (Bequeathed by Sir A.W. Franks)
59 P&E 1907,0520.1 (Given by J. Pierpont Morgan)
61 ME 1928,1010.8
62 ME 1972,0617.2
63 (top) P&E 1893,0715.1 (Given by Sir A.W. Franks) (bottom) P&E 1994,0407.1 (Purchased with the assistance of the Art Fund)
64 (left) The Museum of National Antiquities, Stockholm (right) P&E 1978,1002.1082 (Given by Professor and Mrs Hull Grundy)
67 GR 1816,0610.19
68 P&E WB.98 (Bequeathed by Baron Ferdinand de Rothschild)
69 P&E 1867,0120.1 (Given by Sir A.W. Franks)
70 ME 1891,0623.5
71 P&E 1986,0401.1–356
72 London Assay Office
73 The Goldsmiths' Company
75 PD 1843,0513.802
76 Boston Museum of Fine Arts
77 Boston Museum of Fine Arts
78 Courtauld Institute of Art

80 Bridgeman Art Library
83 Bridgeman Art Library
85 P&E 1850,0601.1–17
86 P&E Eu2002,05.1
87 AES 1919,0208.119
88 (left) P&E 1825,1112.1 (right) AES 1891,0509.84
89 (left) ME 1939,0313.1 (right) AOA Af.6754 (Given by the Revd Greville John Chester)
90 CM 1983,1017.15
91 (left) ASIA 1992,1214.14 (Given by Johannes Nikolaus Schmitt and Mareta Meade) (right) GR 1891,0627.3
92 (left) P&E 1968,1206.1 (Purchased with the assistance of the Art Fund) (right) P&E 1893,0518.3 (Given by Leonard L. Cohen)
93 (left) P&E 1975,1002.18 (right) P&E 1975,1002.6
94 P&E 1975,1002.1–27
95 P&E 1866,1229.1
96 The Brook Club
97 The Mercers' Company
99 CM 1892,1008.11 (Given by Lt-Col. Sir R.C. Temple)
101 London Assay Office
102 London Assay Office
103 London Assay Office
104 London Assay Office
105 (left) London Assay Office (right) The Goldsmiths' Company
108 London Assay Office
109 London Assay Office
110 London Assay Office
112 London Assay Office

Index